A
Slip of
the Pen

A Slip of the Pen

The Writers' Book of Blunders

PETER HAINING

ROBSON BOOKS

This edition first published in Great Britain in 2004 by Robson Books, The Chrysalis Building, Bramley Road, London W10 6SP

An imprint of Chrysalis Books Group plc

British Library Cataloguing in Publication Data
A catalogue record for this title is available from the British Library.

ISBN 1 86105 793 8

Typeset by SX Composing DTP, Rayleigh, Essex
Printed and bound by Clays Ltd, Bungay, Suffolk NR35 1ED

When once the itch of literature comes over a man,
nothing can cure it but the scratching of a pen.

Samuel Lover (1797–1868)

From this it is clear how much the pen is worse than the sword.

Robert Burton (1577–1640)

This book is dedicated to all those who make their living from the pen — except one*

* *My friends will know who I mean.*

Contents

Foreword

Recently I came across a quote by the sixteenth-century French essayist Michel Montaigne in his article 'Of Experience', which said, 'There are more books upon books than upon any other subject.' That is a pretty daunting thought when you are about to add another to the list almost five hundred years later. The truth is, of course, that every generation has loved its books, from the classics to contemporary fact and fiction, and when we are not reading them, what is more interesting than discussing them and their authors? Certainly the act of literary creation demands talent, energy and dedication – Douglas Adams, the late and much-lamented author of *The Hitch-Hiker's Guide to the Galaxy*, once referred to the process as 'staring at a blank piece of paper until your forehead bleeds.' Louis de Bernières, whose best-seller *Captain Corelli's Mandolin*, made him wealthy and famous, offered an even stranger piece of verbal imagery. 'Writing today,' he said, 'is like being stood naked in Trafalgar Square and being told to get an erection.'

Behind the humour of both remarks there is a very real acknowledgement that authorship is bloody difficult, demands a big effort and is full of pitfalls and pratfalls – not the least of them the errors that can occur between the author's manuscript and the published work. That, in a nutshell (and I'm not apologising for the cliché), is what *A Slip of the Pen* is all about.

During my writing career, spanning almost half a century as a newspaper reporter, journalist, publisher and full-time author, I have had a passion for collecting the misdemeanours, unintentional or otherwise, of my chosen profession. And as a result of those years scouring the printed page I have been able to assemble a collection of authors' errors, publishers' boobs, printers' devils, double entendres, comic first lines, weird titles, literary graffiti and howlers, mistranslations, critics' gaffs and all manner of slips committed to paper since the days of Montaigne and even earlier. The book is also something of an autobiography as its contents have grown through the years of my writing life, with its changes in tastes, styles and printing technology – all supposedly for the best – and these are reflected in the different chapters.

Another bestselling contemporary author, Terry Pratchett, whose *Discworld* novels have made him a household name, has been asked countless times (as many authors are) where he gets the ideas for his books. Terry typically replies, 'There's this warehouse called Ideas Are Us . . .' My answer in this instance, though, is less tongue-in-cheek and more straightforward. *A Slip of the Pen* has come from many of those books Montaigne mentioned – as well as a lifetime devoted to reading about books and their authors. I am very grateful to them all, for without them . . .

There is a further quote that I believe is particularly apt as far as this book is concerned. The great Russian writer and critic, Vasili Rozanov, made it not long before his death in 1919. 'The secret of authorship,' he said, 'is in the tips of the fingers.' Antonia Fraser, the historian and novelist, claimed not so long ago that she had an infallible way of ensuring this happened: 'I paint my fingers with nail varnish when they won't seem to write – it always does the trick.' It is when those fingers slip, though, whether using a pen, pencil, typewriter or word processor, that authors create some of the best lines of humour.

Peter Haining,
Suffolk, May 2004

One

Strange Whiskers in the Ear

The Riter's Wrold According to QWERTYUIOP

If I tell you that when my very first story was published some fifty years ago, it was full of literals, the title was changed and – to make things worse – even my name was spelt wrongly, you will no doubt understand why I have had a life-long interest in printers' errors, publishers' mistakes and slips of the writer's pen. Of course, when I became a young newspaper reporter in the fifties, I soon learned just how easy it was for such errors to occur.

You have only to glance at the keyboard of a typewriter (word processor to the younger of my readers) to see how, for example, one wrong touch on the top line, QWERTYUIOP, and you can be in a whole world of trouble, especially with *certain* words, as the pages of this book will reveal time and again. The mistake can be compounded if it slips by an editor and then past the typesetter. In days of yore, typesetting machines produced lines of text from hot metal and if the compositor made an error there was no going back – no rubber, no Tipp-Ex (white-out), no computer spell-check to rite the rong. The whole line had to be reset and the old 'slug' (as they were appropriately named) consigned to the melting pot. On a great many occasions, though, they slithered into print . . . and then the fun began.

Collecting newspaper misprints is certainly not a new pursuit. As long ago as 1884, Frederic Williams, a London journalist with a wicked sense of humour produced a little book, *Journalistic Jumbles: or, Trippings in Type*, which he sub-titled, 'Being Notes on some Newspaper Blunders, their Origin and Nature' and included numerous examples, with a typical Victorian's eye for decency. Another newspaperman, W W Scott, had no such inhibitions when in 1931 he produced *Breaks*, 'A Collection of Mistakes and Misprints by those associated with the Newspaper, Magazine and Book Racket'. A copy of this volume with its comical illustrations by Nate Collier was given to me on the day I became a journalist by an uncle who was a second-hand book dealer. It was probably intended as a salutary warning, but it certainly provided hours of amusing reading. Later still, in the fifties, another whimsical fellow, Denys Parsons, followed in the footsteps of Williams and Scott and continued to scour the pages of national and local newspapers to compile a number of collections during the next thirty years.

Although I worked on a newspaper and then a London trade journal during the early years of my career, my particular interest was always in the slips of the pen and ink in magazine short stories and books – the area of publishing in which I hoped eventually to work. Consequently, it was the faux pas of authors, the literals that somehow escaped the blue pencils of sub editors, and the gibberish perpetrated by printers that caught my eye, and it is the best of these amusing and often risqué misprints that form this opening chapter.

After having given vent to this beautiful reflection,
Mr Pickwick proceeded to put himself into his clothes;
and his clothes into his portmanteau.

> Charles Dickens, *Pickwick Papers*

Time had rolled back a hundred years. People hurrying office-wards in the Strand waved their hats and raised a cheer to the immoral memory of Mr Pickwick.

> Arthur Ramsey, *London Tapestry*

The Nolotic race is remarkable for the disproportionately long legs of their women. They extend on the eastern side of the Nile right down into the Uganda Protectorate.

> Max Pemberton, *Strange Travels in Strange Places*

I was terrified. There was the tiger crouching, ready to bounce.

> Fred M White, 'An Object Lesson'

'I love you, too,' she cried, and swaying toward him, threw herself into his arms. His lips found and clung to her sweet, tremendous mouth.

> Elizabeth Banks, 'How the Debt Was Paid'

His disappointment was keen, yet in after days he looked upon the evening as that date on which he burst from the chrysalis and became a caterpillar.

> E Lynn Linton, *The World Well Lost*

'I didn't know that you cared for me that way,' she said. 'I've always thought of you as just a great big bother.'

> Jean Ingelow, *Lost and Won*

With an effort, Jean pulled herself together. She stopped crying and dried her ears.

Helen Mathers, 'A Summer Girl

She picked up a snapshot of a dear friend who had recently died on her bedroom mantelpiece

Kate Field, 'A Woman's World

For the chief the word compromise had no meaning. He answered his men in violet language.

Frederick Boyle, *A Story of the Transvaa*

Mrs Gale patted his arm affectionately. 'Don't forget,' she said, 'Come and hook me up next Thursday.'

Thomas Arthur, 'The Wayward Wife

'Mr Perkins might be able to help you,' she said, as she took down a dusty lodger from the shelf.

James Payn, *Winifred's Lovers*

'Why are you here today, Mr Lomax?' Alice stumbled over the familiar name. Mark reached out his hand to help her to her feet

Marjorie Bowen, 'My Lady Played

I must say that when at last the house was completed, it was an awful shack to us.

Marian Carter, *The Retrea*

There were two sharp reports and Radley lunched and staggered.

Wilson McCoy, *The G-Mar*

When he refused to give any evidence to the police he was charged with assault and carrying a gnu.

Frank Holderness, *The Silent Stranger*

The skipper spat disconsolately down the engine-room ventilator and stopped the engines.

W W Jacobs, *Dangerous Waters*

They had hardly got into the skipper's cabin when a tremendous pitch on the steamer sent Leila rolling on the floor. Before she could be got under control again she had shipped hundreds of tons of water. Then her nose went down and her tail went up and for a moment it was a question if she would right herself. A wiggle and a roll and she saved herself.

Albert Wetjen, *Afloat*

'If you ask me,' said Doris, 'it's more like twelve years they have been married. I don't think they will ever have a chill now.'

Eleanor Stuart, 'The Right Man'

My father was born in poor circumstances, but he did a rich man.

Katherine Tynan, *A Bit of a Scandal*

From his left ear to the corner of his mouth ran a long scar, the result of a duet many years before.

William le Queux, *Flight from Germany*

For a moment he stood there looking into her eyes.
Between them was a bowl of hyacinths.

Elizabeth Robins, *Under the Southern Cross*

'The Duchess still looks quite a girl,'
she said, 'and so does the Duke,
particularly now that he has
shaven off his tiny moustache.'

Louis Cohen, 'The Mayfair Set'

He leaned his head against her hair. A wasp strayed
across his face. He kissed it.

Alison Bold, *Moments to Cherish*

Pierre fingered one of his ears caressingly and looked thoughtfully
at the other.

Paul Renin, *One Night in Paris*

Then it spread to Liz, who clapped a hand over her
mouth above blue eyes that watered with silent laughter.

Henry Green, *Nothing*

She covered her face with her hands and cried brokenly.
But, coming closer, he put both hands on her shoulders
and lifted her tea-stained face to his.

Marilyn Foster, 'A Heart on Fire'

John Godfrey gathered the pale and
wistful face into one hand,
crumpling it up ridiculously, then
he kissed it all over, released it and
put her head back on his waistcoat,
smoothing her rumpled hair.

Raymond Ellis, *The Girl from the Country*

Their house was full of little birds and I can see them to this day sitting on the sofa, holding hands and beaming.

Beth Cheney, *A Rural Idyll*

The eminent statistician rubbed his ear thoughtfully and produced a cigarette.

W Clark Russell, 'In Troubled Times'

She stood at the foot of the stairs, narrowing her eyes and breathing deeply through her hips.

Jennifer Mason, *The Moment is Past*

Deeply troubled, he wrote a poem about the war and the fighting hen.

William J Ford, *One Brave Soldier*

It wasn't the proper doctor — just a young locust taking his place while he was away.

Felix Barker, 'Heartbreak Hospital'

'You look a bit washed out, Bill,' said Doreen. She walked across the room and put her arm through him.

John Oxenham, *The Black Opal*

She sat huddled in a chair, covering her ears with crossed legs.

Edgar Jepson, 'The Moment of Truth'

As he uttered the important word he dropped his voice, but she just managed to catch it.

Amy Ferguson, *The Unexpected Witness*

Raymond was perfectly happy. He loved this woman with a great and growling love.

Ian Maclaren, 'A Glasgow Drama'

The faces of the two men were livid with rage as she quietly crumpled them up and threw them on the fire.

Ella Fuller Maitland, *Christmas Expectations*

It was one of those perfect June nights that so seldom occur except in August.

Frankfort Moore, 'Reggie's Rival'

Miss Sutton struck out in all directions and the nurses called for help. However, when Dr Jackling arrived she had been overpowdered.

Winifred Holtby, *Nothing to Fear*

The half-starved man sat down at the rough deal table and began to eat it ravenously.

Anthony Hope, *Bad Matches*

Anne crept cautiously up the stairs and knocked timidly at the door with the jelly.

Violet Hunt, *Window on the World*

He put the melting honey-coloured fruit on her plate and got out a silk handkerchief. She began to eat it thoughtfully.

F C Phillips, 'Romance for the Chambermaid'

Later that same evening after a vain search all around the village, Mary found the dog dead in the garden. She curried the body indoors.

Patricia Cox, *Life in Barnsthorpe*

she was sorry she had agreed to
sleep in the haunted house, because
all night long she was troubled by
strange whiskers in her ear.

Edith A Barnett, 'The Haunted House'

Ted could not raise the cash necessary to purchase a house, and eventually in desperation he had to burrow.

Rosemary Jeans, *The Price of Love*

They looked out of the window as the train drew into Crewe station. 'Hull!' they cried, 'we're there.'

David Partridge, 'The Thompsons' Holiday'

The Phyllida *throbbed with whispering engines to the shining, wet landing stage. Thorne caught her lightly and half lifted her ashore. 'By Jove, you're wet!' he said.*

Stanley Weyman, *Phyllida*

'I am certain of one thing.
Whatever may come between us –
and wherever he may be on earth –
Arthur will always remember that
I love ham.

Millicent Hemming, *The Parting*

She had a pleasant voice, more like her smile than her sneer, but the man was frightened by an English voice and he submerged himself in his soup.

Warwick Deeping, *Restitution*

I never went through that ghastly adolescent phase most girls experience. I went from child to woman in one go. One day I was a child. The next a man.

Patricia Gowling, 'A Hard Woman'

Sir Harry had his top lip caught under his lower teeth.

W L Alden, *The Precedent*

My teeth were chattering as with a
fever chill, when they all tumbled out.

Roy Trevor, *The Deserted Wood*

Marjorie would often take her eyes from the deck and cast them far out to sea.

Ursula Bloom, *A Voyage of Discovery*

He bent swiftly and found her lips and, without removing them from her mouth, lifted her to her feet and drew her into his arms.

Sonia Deane, *There is a Destiny*

'You don't care,' she accused him. 'You don't care whether I do or not.' The trembling lips resolved themselves into two bright tears that gathered on the edges of her eyelids.

Beatrice Haraden, *Tragedy for Sarah*

The door opened and a girl
came in – a slip of a girl
with a firm little chin and a
pair of lively grey ewes which
gave Bernard a searching glance.

Thomas Prescott, The *Guardian*

Alice paused and, to hide her confusion, busied herself adjusting ornaments on the mantelpiece which needed no adjustment. Then she turned her sweet, flour-like face towards him.

Marjorie Golden, 'Uncertainty'

He had been aware from the first that she was unusually attractive. Now, in her dark green dress with the low-cut, rounded neckline, he saw that she had lovely legs.

G H Coxe, *The Jade Venus*

Once again for an instant she raised those wonderful eyes to his. He studied the thickness of the lashes as they fell once more to her lap.

Barbara Cartland, *Love Will Triumph*

The doctor looked closely at the woman's face. 'It's a most peculiar thing,' he murmured.

Winifred Tanner, 'Reflections'

Elizabeth found herself on a stool by the nursery fire. Securely pierced by a long brass toasting fork she held a square of bread to the glowing flameless fire.

Jane MacDonald, *The Tides of Love*

He said he had a full and exciting wife.

James Edmunds, *The Story of Tom*

The lady in the thin black dress and a widow's veil, turned away and with a curling lip began to turn over a book lying on a table near her.

Roland James, 'The Mystery at Fetters'

Without a word Esther slid to the floor with a bullet through her false heart.

Darcy Glinto, *Death in New York*

Involuntarily, Max's eyes followed the length of the prostrate form, then uttered a piercing scream.

Peter Preston, *The Girl in the Club*

What was the meaning of all that apparatus? Racks of test tubes, most of them half-full; the microscopes on stands; the Bunsen burners; the white-painted box, on which was the word Incubator — what were these things? In a flash of intuition, Creighton realised the truth. He was in a laboratory.

James Corbett, *The Somerville Case*

'The cause of death is a mystery,' the detective said, 'no doctor was attending him at the time.'

Frank McShane, 'With Murder in Mind'

'I'll tell you what you are,' cried Slim. 'You're as crooked as a corkscrew — and that's straight!'

Peter Cheyney, *A Case for Callaghan*

In one corner of the room, square tins of every shape were piled.

Edgar Wallace, *The Talkative Burglar*

'Today,' she said, and he held up a thumb and grinned at her. If only this could be for ever, the two of them alone. But the sea lifted the boat like a sullen cork and he stopped thinking about anything but handling her.

Richard Miles, *Exiled to the Pacific*

He glanced at May. She wasn't knitting, but sat there, looking down at the floor, with knitted brows.
        W Somerset Maugham, 'The Hour Before the Dawn'

The three girls spent several days at home with their mother. It was the first time the neighbours had the pleasure of seeing them in the altogether at one time.
        Flora A Steel, *Long Island Days*

Riley sat at the back, with Miss Blandish lying on his feet, biting his nails.

James Hadley Chase, *No Orchids for Miss Blandish*

The dame walked close to me, and it was obvious that underneath her clothing she wore little or nothing.

Hank Janson, *Hotsy – You'll Be Chilled*

She had dark red hair and a fair skin which she told me came out in a mass of freckles at the first hint of sin.

Paul Mason, *City Without Justice*

I felt my hair being yanked cruelly as I tumbled to the ground. Aubrey's hate-crazed face hoovered over me.

Morton Cooper, *Confessions of a Striptease Artist*

From childhood to manhood, Julia and Harry lost no time in engaging in amorous adventures.

Christopher Lewis, *Past Redemption*

Catherine had always been lucky. Even the sun was shining when she first saw it.

Martin Hummerstone, 'Distant Horizons'

She would get new dresses, new bathing-costumes, new everything. She would have a glorious bust.

Rachel Wing, 'Joy for Amanda'

On the floor above him lived a redheaded instructor in physical education, whose muscular calves he admired when they nodded to each other, by the mailbox.

E V Cunningham, *Sally*

He sat in the little flat in Chelsea blissfully eating crumpets over which Emily had spread the preposterous amount of butter which proceeds from an overflowing heart.

John Regardie, 'Story of Three Lives'

slowly, almost one by one, Ordway's eyes followed the new steps in the snow.

Hammond Innes, *The White Tower*

The doctor smiled reassuringly at the worried mother and patted her little bot on the cheek.

Josephine Lawrence, *Prescription for Love*

She was a very neurotic woman with one leg in this world and the other in a world of her own. 'Between these two she doesn't know quite where she is,' said her solicitor.

Arthur Steward, 'The Circle of Mystery'

The ultimate pay-off line in a sex novel after all the years of drawing a veil or a row of dots over the bedroom action, probably occurred in Rosemary Cockburn's 1976 novel, *Happiness Tomorrow*:

He smiled and let his gaze fall to hers, so that her cheek began to glow.
Ecstatically she waited until his mouth neared her own.
She knew only one thing then.
Qwertyuiop asdfghjkl zxcvbnm.

It was a Dark and Stormy Night . . .

Bad Beginnings and Worse Sex

I learned one of the most basic lessons of writing, 'How to Begin a Story', when I was still a young journalist. It was given to me – sometimes painfully for my ego and often for my respiratory system – by a fiery, bearded, pipe-smoking Scottish sub editor. Without a word of warning, he would hurl my copy back at me shouting (most of the expletives now deleted), 'Mr Haining [he called everyone on the paper 'Mister'] you've missed the f*****g intro!' What he meant was that my opening paragraph was not sufficiently attention-grabbing to seize the interest of readers and make them want to continue. In all probability, the intro – that vital nugget of journalistic gold – would be found three or four paragraphs into my report and, once installed in its rightful place, would provoke another response from the glowering Scotsman. Not, I hasten to add, a word of praise, but a blast of foul-smelling tobacco smoke expelled through his pursed lips in my direction. It was enough, though, to let me know that I had got the story right at last.

Catching the reader's interest in books is, if anything, even more difficult – and again, what happens on the first page can have a very big influence. Some writers have turned this into a fine art and others have always had a problem. Charles Dickens, for one, often struggled trying to get his story off the ground, which could seriously damage the potential of his work as it invariably first appeared in serial form. Indeed, he delivered one classic 'How Not to Do It' opening line for *Little Dorritt* (1855). 'Thirty years ago,' he wrote, 'Marseilles lay burning in the sun, one day.' He might have taken a leaf from the start of Franz Kafka's 'The Metamorphosis' – if the Czech author had been alive half a century earlier, of course – which begins, 'As Gregor Samsa awoke one morning from uneasy dreams, he found himself transformed in his bed into a gigantic insect.' Now *that* should make you want to read on.

In this chapter I have selected some of the best opening lines in literature. I have also included a number of other extracts from books that reveal the amusing and sometimes excruciating lengths authors have gone to in order to hold their readers' attention. Apart from these 'page turners' (on or off, the choice is there to be made), I have inserted (if you will pardon the expression) some of the most hilarious sex scenes in popular fiction – an undertaking that has resulted in any number of pratfalls (ditto) for the world's novelists. Among these selections are the winners of the 'Bad Sex Fiction Award' instituted in 1993 by Auberon Waugh, then editor of the *Literary Review*. This 'most dreaded literary honour' – to quote *The Times* – is given annually for the most crude, tasteless and often perfunctory 'bit of the other' in a novel. You have been warned!

The title of the chapter, incidentally, is taken from the opening paragraph of a notorious, rambling Victorian saga, *Paul Clifford*, which since 1982 has been the inspiration for another annual fiction competition run by San Jose State

University for the 'opening sentence of the worst of all possible novels'.

A mistress should be like a little country retreat near the town; not to dwell in constantly, but only for a night and away!

William Wycherley, *The Country Wife* (1675)

She suddenly uttered a long and piercing shriek as he seized her. She appeared to be taken with an excess of delirium; she tore her hair, beat her bosom, used the most frantic gestures, and drawing a poniard from her girdle, plunged it into her.

Matthew Lewis, *The Monk* (1795)

It is a truth universally acknowledged that a single man in possession of a good fortune, must be in want of a wife.

Jane Austen, *Pride and Prejudice* (1813)

It was a dark and stormy night, the rain fell in torrents — except at occasional intervals, when it was checked by a violent gust of wind which swept up the streets (for it is in London that our scene lies), rattling along the housetops and fiercely agitating the scanty flame of the lamps that struggled against the darkness.

Edward Bulwer-Lytton, *Paul Clifford* (1830)

In the year 1775, there stood upon the borders of Epping Forest, at a distance of about twelve miles from London — measuring from the Standard in Cornhill or rather from the spot on or near to which the Standard

used to be in days of yore – a house of public
entertainment called The Maypole.

Charles Dickens, *Barnaby Rudge* (1841)

'Barbara! Barbara!' he ejaculated. 'I have seen Thorn! Every drop of
blood within me began to tingle, and an impulse came upon me to
spring upon him and accuse him of the murder.'

Mrs Henry Wood, *East Lynne* (1861)

One thing was certain, that was
the white kitten had had nothing
to do with it – it was the black
kitten's fault entirely.

Lewis Carroll, *Through the Looking-Glass* (1872)

I am nothing to you. I know I never touched a fibre of
your heart or fancy. But better would it be for you to love
a man dead in a coffin, than to love one to whom at any
hour the law may snatch from you and send to fret his
years away in the horrors of prison.

Ouida (Louise Ramé), *In Maremma* (1882)

Buck did not read the newspapers or he would have known that trouble
was brewing, not alone for himself, but for every tidewater dog, strong
of muscle and with warm, long hair, from Puget Sound to San Diego.

Jack London, *Call of the Wild* (1903)

The human race, to which so many of my readers belong.

G K Chesterton, *The Napoleon of Notting Hill* (1904)

Once upon a time and a very good time it was there was
a moocow coming down along the road and this moocow
that was coming down along the road met a nicens little
boy named baby tuckoo.

James Joyce, *Portrait of the Artist as a Young Man* (1917)

Henry Lakington is the second most dangerous man in London.

Sapper, *Bull-Dog Drummond* (1920)

His body vibrated taut and powerful as he closed upon her and crushed her, breathless and dazed and destroyed, crushed her upon his breast. Ah, it was terrible and perfect.

D H Lawrence, *Women in Love* (1920)

I believe that a well-known anecdote exists to the effect that a young writer, determined to make the commencement of his story forcible and original enough to catch and rivet the attention of the most blasé of editors, penned the following sentence: 'Hell!' said the Duchess.'

Agatha Christie, *The Murder on the Links* (1923)

'Sent down for indecent behaviour, eh?' said Paul Pennyfeather's guardian.

Evelyn Waugh, *Decline and Fall* (1928)

Some things can't be ravished. You can't ravish a tin of sardines.

D H Lawrence, *Lady Chatterly's Lover* (1928)

He spent his declining years trying to guess the answer to the Irish question. Unfortunately, whenever he was getting warm, the Irish secretly changed the question.

W C Sellar & R J Yeatman, *1066 And All That* (1930)

'Damn, I'm late,' Bernard said to himself as he first caught sight of Big Henry, the Singery clock.

Aldous Huxley, *Brave New World* (1932)

Names and descriptions of Broadcasting House have
varied from the complimentary to the scurrilous. It has
been called a worthy edifice well fitted to the marvels it
contains to a damned awful erection.

Val Gielgud, *Death at Broadcasting House* (1934)

Hale knew, before he had been in
Brighton three hours, that they
meant to murder him.

Graham Greene, *Brighton Rock* (1938)

I am a camera with its shutter open, quite passive,
recording, not thinking.

Christopher Isherwood, *Goodbye to Berlin* (1939)

Gee! Only one woman a year, and that a dead 'un!

Jonathan Latimer, *Naboth's Vineyard* (1943)

When Mrs Frederick C Little's second son
arrived, everybody noticed that he was not much bigger
than a mouse.

E H White, *Stuart Little* (1945)

Bang! Bang! Bang! Three shots in
the groin and I was off on the
greatest adventure of my life.

Thomas Kingston, *Sleep Till Noon* (1946)

I guess I'm just an old mad scientist at bottom. Give
me an underground laboratory, half a dozen atom
smashers, and a beautiful girl in a diaphanous veil
waiting to be turned into a chimpanzee, and I care not
who writes the nation's laws.

S J Perelman, *One Touch of Venus* (1948)

It was a bright cold day in April and the clocks were striking thirteen.

George Orwell, *Nineteen Eighty-Four* (1949)

SECOND MILLION   PRICE ONE PENNY

WILL THE OLD BOOK STAND?

By
H. L. Hastings

LONDON
MARSHALL BROTHERS - 10, PATERNOSTER ROW.

If you really want to hear about it, the first thing you'll probably want to know is where I was born, and what my lousy childhood was like, and how my parents were occupied and all before they had me, and all of that David Copperfield kind of crap.

J D Salinger, *The Catcher in the Rye* (1951)

I write this sitting in the kitchen sink.

Dodie Smith, *I Capture the Castle* (1952)

The past is a foreign country: they do things differently there.

L P Hartley, *The Go-Between* (1953)

The scene and smoke and sweat of a casino are nauseating at three in the morning.

Ian Fleming, *Casino Royale* (1953)

'There's such a thing as the Chastity of Women Act, which prevents one speaking out. And I've no wish to take away another's character, even if she does move in high society where those things don't matter.

Honor Tracy, *The Deserters* (1954)

Lolita, light of my life, fire of my loins, my sin, my soul.

Vladimir Nabokov, *Lolita* (1955)

Wynstan's arms tightened as she spoke. 'I am not . . . really sure . . . about what men and women . . . do when they . . . make love . . . but it must be . . . wonderful . . .'

Barbara Cartland, *No Time For Love* (1956)

Nothing happens, nobody comes, nobody goes. It's awful.

Samuel Beckett, *Waiting for Godot* (1956)

They're out there.
Ken Kesey, *One Flew Over the Cuckoo's Nest* (1960)

David arrived at Coetminais the afternoon after the one he had landed at Cherbourg and driven down to Avarnaches, where he had spent the intervening Tuesday night.

John Fowles, *The Collector* (1963)

I'm going to get that bloody bastard if I die in the attempt.

James Clavell, *King Rat* (1965)

Many years later, as he faced the firing squad, Colonel Aureliano Buendía was to remember that distant afternoon when his father took him to discover ice.

Gabriel García Marquéz, *One Hundred Years of Solitude* (1967)

It was love at first sight.

Joseph Heller, *Catch 22* (1968)

What can you say about a twenty-five-year-old girl who died?

Eric Segal, *Love Story* (1968)

It all began so suddenly. The reptilian forces of Megenth, long quiescent, suddenly began to expand due to the serum given them by Charles Engstrom, the power-crazed telepath.

Robert Sheckley, *Zirn Left Unguarded* (1969)

Death was a grim business in the Middle Ages.

Thomas Boase, *Death in the Middle Ages* (1972)

There were 117 psychoanalysts on the Pam Am flight to Vienna and I'd been treated by at least six of them.

Erica Jong, *Fear of Flying* (1973)

I can see by my watch, without taking my hand from the left grip of the cycle, that it is eight-thirty in the morning.

Robert M Pirsig, *Zen and the Art of Motorcycle Maintenance* (1974)

I want a sense of purpose in my life. I don't want to die in Chelsea with my knickers down.

Jilly Cooper, *Emily* (1975)

Even before the deal with Straker had been consummated (that's some word all right, he thought, and his eyes crawled over the front of his secretary's blouse), Lawrence Crockett was, without doubt, the richest man in Salem's Lot and one of the richest in Cumberland County, although there was nothing about his office or his person to indicate it.

Stephen King, *Salem's Lot* (1975)

One of the things Ford Prefect had always found hardest to understand about human beings was their habit of continually stating or repeating the obvious, as in 'it's a nice day,' or 'you're very tall,' or 'oh, dear, you seem to have fallen down a 30ft well.'

Douglas Adams, *The Hitch-Hiker's Guide to the Galaxy* (1979)

It was the afternoon of my eighty-first birthday, and I was in bed with my catamite when Ali announced that the archbishop had come to see me.

Anthony Burgess, *Earthly Powers* (1980)

As they lay together, half asleep,
but unwilling to drift apart into
unconsciousness, Daisy farted, in a
tiny series of absolutely irrepressible
little pops that seemed to her to go
on for a minute.

Judith Krantz, *Princess Daisy* (1980)

The blood that had abandoned her countenance rushed
into his.

Elizabeth Peters, *The Lion in the Valley* (1986)

I intensely disliked my father's fifth wife, but not to the point of
murder.

Dick Francis, *Hot Money* (1987)

She wanted to wrap her legs around him the way a tree
wraps itself around a mountain.

Jan Stacy, *Bodysmasher* (1988)

By the end of the alley, the fine
hairs in my nostrils were starting
to twitch.

Lindsay Davis, *Shadows in Bronze* (1990)

She wore a dress the same color as her eyes her father
brought her from San Francisco.

Danielle Steel, *Star* (1993)

Their jaws ground in feverish mutual mastication. Saliva
and sweat. Sweat and saliva. There was a purposeful
shedding of clothes.

Philip Hook, *The Stonebreakers* (1994)

His tremulous thumbs gathered the elastic waist of her panties and plucked them down over the twin golden domes of her behind and back up the suspended sentences and Sobranie filtered tips of her stocking tops. Detached mind from over-eager gnomen and its exquisitely appointed, shadowy task, he began to make love to her. When they had finished they lay under the sheet and watched TV.

Philip Kerr, *Gridiron* (1995)

As Jean-Claude explored her body with his own, teased and titillated her with his lips and tongue, she felt an explosion of such intensity that it made her body shake. She also felt an enormous outpouring of love. She had pretended for years that she didn't need it, or want it. And so it began.

Joan Collins, *Too Damn Famous* (1995)

He was as guarded as a virgin, but infinitely more experienced.

Cathy Spellman, *An Excess of Love* (1996)

Eighteen years ago on the night of her eighth birthday, in a seaside cottage on Key West, Chyna had squirmed under her bed to hide from Jim Woltz, her mother's friend. A storm had been raging from the Gulf of Mexico, and the sky-blistering lightning had made her fearful of escaping the sanctuary of the beach where she'd retreated on other nights. After committing herself to the cramped space under the iron bed, which had been lower slung than this one, she had discovered that she was sharing it with a palmetto beetle.

Dean Koontz, *Intensity* (1996)

'Stick it in,' she whispered. I moved up the bed and pushed inside her. Liz squeaked like wet rubber. She grabbed my love handles and ground her hips against me, her eyes black saucers, staring into mine as she hooked a yoga-leg onto my shoulder. We went through a medley of our favourite positions.

David Huggins, *The Big Kiss* (1996)

I remember the first time I travelled on Concorde. I was totally in awe of the number of internationally famous faces on board and it was some time before I noticed the passengers were in fact casting surreptitious glances at me. It was then that it dawned on me that mine was the most famous face of all.

Naomi Campbell, *Swan* (1996)

We were making out all the way up her stairs; as we got inside her apartment, we just started screwing. She stopped me, got up naked and walked to the bathroom and started to vomit.

Ethan Hawke, *The Hottest State* (1997)

Yasmin grinned and writhed on the bed, arching her back, making a noise somewhere between a beached seal and a police siren.

Nicholas Royle, *The Matter of the Heart* (1997)

The knife was poised above her heart. Her screams cut through the dead, rotten air of the warehouse. Batiste Legendre smiled. He bent down and soul-kissed the terrified eighteen-year-old who was to remain that age forever.

Vincent Courtney, *Vampire Beat* (1998)

His hands stroked her shoulders and arms, then slid the Lycra top off her waist revealing her perfectly formed breasts. By the time they had slipped naked under the duvet he was lost in the warmth and fragrant passion of Lisa Drake.

Alan Titchmarsh, *Mr MacGregor* (1998)

Meanwhile her ears were filled with the sound of a soft but frantic gasping and it was some time before she identified it as her own.

Sebastian Faulks, *Charlotte Gray* (1998)

The rash-rubbed thighs clamped cheeks, bits of liverish flesh draped across his nose and coarse hair scraped his chin. There seemed to be such a lot of her.

A A Gill, *Starcrossed* (1999)

All was chaos. In the universe of James T Kirk his bride lay dying, their unborn child within her. In the plasma storms of the Badlands, three starships held an impossible portal open to another reality.

William Shatner, *Star Trek: Preserver* (2000)

Her small white body. She is so small and compact, and yet she has all the necessary features. Shall I compare thee to a Sony Walkman, thou art more compact and more. She is his own Toshiba, his dinky little JVC, his sweet Aiwa.

Sean Thomas, *Kissing England* (2000)

He brings his body up next to hers.
Mirabelle, foetal, curled up like a
bug, receives the proximity of Ray
Porter as though it were a
nourishing stream. They wake in
the morning on either side of
the bed.

Steve Martin, *Shopgirl* (2000)

Her hand is moving away from my knee and heading
north. Heading unnervingly and with a steely will
towards the pole. And like Sir Ranulph Fiennes,
Pamela will not easily be discouraged.

Christopher Hart, *Rescue Me* (2001)

Professor Malik Solanka, retired historian of ideas, irascible dollmaker,
and since his recent fifty-fifth birthday, celibate and solitary by his own
(much criticized) choice, in his silvered years found himself living in a
golden age.

Salman Rushdie, *Fury* (2001)

And then he was fully socketed to her, like a pipe wrench
in a crock of warm chilli.

Robert Tanenbaum, *Act of Revenge* (2001)

She felt herself aching with the
furtive control she had taken over
him. If she were to take some
pleasure of him while he slept, he
need never know.

Sebastian Faulks, *On Green Dolphin Street* (2001)

I was 21 years old, queer and a Buckingham Palace footman in 1967 when, for the first time, I found myself drawn to a political figure who was neither Lady Violet Bonham-Carter or Bessie Braddock.

Guy Hunting, *Adventures of a Gentleman's Gentleman* (2002)

She popped the elastic at the top of the second sock and pushed her sexually ambiguous Timex watch up along the blond hairs of her handsome forearms.

Steve Whalen, *A Love Story* (2002)

His head has been pushed down into the dusty bedclothes, so he cannot see the purple face of the man toiling behind him. He is aware, however, that the pounding is punctuated by buttock-slaps and regular full-throated hunting cries as the major's excitement mounts. 'Tally-ho!' gives way to 'On! On! On!' and the bed groans with the effort of maintaining its structural integrity.

Hari Kunzru, *The Impressionist* (2002)

She closed her eyes, saw his dark-as-treacle-toffee eyes gazing down at her. Weirdly, he was clad in pinstripes at the same time as being naked. Pinstripes were erotic, the uniform of fathers, two-dimensional fathers. Even his penis had a seductive pinstriped foreskin.

Wendy Perrian, *Tread Softly* (2002)

When he finally came, it was like dropping a naked electric cable into a fish tank.

Nicholas Blincoe, *White Mice* (2002)

She is topping up your engine oil for the cross-country coming up. Your RPM is hitting a new high. To wait any longer would be to lose prime time. She picks up a Bugatti's momentum. You want her more at a Volkswagen's steady trot. Squeeze the maximum mileage out of your gallon of gas. But she's eating up the road with all cylinders blazing.

Aniruddha Bahalm, Bunker 13 (2003)

Many last lines of books are also memorable in the same kind of absurd or humorous way. As a taster, here are two of my favourites. The first is from Percy Shelley's *The Cenci* which closes with, 'And yours, I see, is coming down'; and the second from Terry Southern and Mason Hoffenburg's *Candy*, with the heroine's startled exclamation, 'Good grief – it's Daddy!'

Three

Hear My Lady Come

A Risqué Choice of Double Entendres

Double entendres, whether intentional or not, can be the bane of any writer's life. In my early days as a reporter in Essex, one of our rivals dropped a hilarious clanger that afforded the rest of us amusement for weeks and became something of a local legend. The story materialised as a result of doubts arising about the holding of the annual beanfeast by the civic dignitaries in a nearby town. Our competitor ran a headline on its front page that was intended to be unequivocal but became something else entirely: MAYOR'S BALL HANGS IN BALANCE. That line of large type must have been read by any number of members of the staff, from the reporter who wrote it to the sub who prepared it for press, and even those in the printworks while it was being proofed for printing. But they all apparently missed the double entendre until the paper hit the streets . . . by which time it was too late to do anything.

The world of books was, I soon discovered, just as prone to such errors, with the great and the good of literature as guilty of perpetrating such gaffs as the lowly hacks. The author Sir John

Betjeman once gave a talk that I covered for my paper and during this told an amusing story about a little boy – himself possibly? – who was fascinated by his grandmother's ability to get wild birds to feed on her windowsill. A pair of blue-tits were so tame that they would take crumbs from her hand. One particular day, said Betjeman with a smile, the boy ran into a room where his parents were entertaining some guests and shrieked with delight, 'Mummy, Daddy, I've just seen Grandmother's tits.' Another popular speaker of the era, Chips Channon, delighted audiences with stories of his love for the novels of Anthony Trollope. 'There's nothing I like better,' he would grin mischievously, 'than lying on my bed for an hour or so with my favourite Trollope.'

So without further ado, here is a selection of the ripest double entendres that I have been able to cull from the pages of our finest authors – a selection where such familiar favourites as Jane Austen, Charles Dickens and Henry James will unwittingly be found among the worst bloomers.

He wants to visit with the head of his hanging piece the familiar hole he has often filled before with its equal length.

Anonymous, *The Key* (c fourteenth century)

I felt, me thought, two fiery balls fly whizzing through my liver,
And Beauty, a bold thief, cried 'Stand – Deliver!'
Giovanni Guarini, *The Pastor Fido* (1585)

How brave a prospect is a bright Back-side!
Henry Vaughan, *Thalia Rediviva: The Pastimes & Diversions of a Country Muse* (1678)

CHARMIAN: Help, chafe her temples, Iras.
IRAS: Bend, bend her forward quickly.
CHARMIAN: Heaven be praised. She comes again.
John Dryden, *All For Love* (1678)

The confidence which presumes to
do, by surveying the surface, what
labour only can perform, by
penetrating the bottom.

Samuel Johnson, *The Rambler* (1748)

Soon after came the Prince of Wales and Prince
Edward; and then the Lady Augusta, all quite
undressed, and they took their stools and sat round the
fire with us.

George Dodington, *Journal* (1754)

I won't go about to argue the point with you — 'tis so — and I am
persuaded of it, madam, as much as can be, 'That both man and
woman bear pain or sorrow (and, for aught I know, pleasure too) best
in a horizontal position.'

Laurence Sterne, *The Life and Opinions of Tristram Shandy* (1759)

I'll come no more behind your scenes, David, for the silk
stockings and white bosoms of your actresses excite my
amorous propensities.

James Boswell, *Life of Samuel Johnson* (1791)

Soon shalt thou hear the
    bridegroom's voice,
The midnight cry, 'Behold, I come!'

James Lowes, *The Midnight Cry* (1800)

I dined at Deane yesterday and met the two Mr Holders. We played at Vingt-un, *which as Fulwar was unsuccessful, gave him an opportunity of exposing himself as usual.*

Jane Austen, *Letters to Cassandra* (1801)

In winter, his private balls were numerous enough for any young lady who was not suffering under the insatiable appetite of fifteen.

Jane Austen, *Sense and Sensibility* (1811)

On entering the drawing-room, she found the whole party at loo and was immediately invited to join them.

Jane Austen, *Pride and Prejudice* (1813)

Mrs Goddard was the mistress of a school – not of a seminary, or an establishment, or anything which professed, in long sentences of refined nonsense to combine liberal acquirements with elegant morality upon new principles and new systems – and where young ladies for enormous pay might be screwed out of health and into vanity.

Jane Austen, *Emma* (1816)

Such was Catherine Morland at ten. At fifteen appearances were mending; she began to cut her hair and long for balls.

Jane Austen, *Northanger Abbey* (1818)

From my window I saw them running through the garden in every direction, embracing each other, ejaculating, playing, and counting their beads, with hands tremulous and eyes uplifted in ecstasy.

Charles Robert Maturin, *Melmoth the Wanderer* (1820)

She touched the organ;
I could stand for hours and hours.

Winthrop Praed, *The Belle of the Ballroom* (1828)

'The curse has come upon me,' cried
The Lady of Shalott.

Alfred, Lord Tennyson *The Lady of Shalott* (1833)

Miss Bolo went straight home, in floods of tears and a sedan chair.

Charles Dickens, *Pickwick Papers* (1836)

Sebald, as we lay,
Rising and falling only with our pants,
Who said, 'Let Death come now – 'tis right to die!'

Robert Browning, *Pippa Passes* (1841)

She touched his organ, and from that bright epoch, even it, the old companion of his happiest hours, incapable as he had thought of elevation, began a new and deified existence.

Charles Dickens, *Martin Chuzzlewit* (1843)

*I deeply appreciate his talent for the organ,
notwithstanding that I do not, if I may use the
expression, grind myself.*

Charles Dickens, *Martin Chuzzlewit* (1843)

'My master,' he says, 'has forewarned me. Daily he
announces more distinctly, "Surely I come quickly"
and hourly I more eagerly respond, "Amen! Even so,
come, Lord Jesus!"'

Charlotte Brontë, *Jane Eyre* (1847)

Miss Sedley's new femme de chambre refused to go to bed without
a wax candle.

William Makepeace Thackeray, *Vanity Fair* (1847–8)

The organ begins to swell;
She's coming, she's coming!
My lady comes at last.

William Makepeace Thackeray, *At the Church Gate* (1854)

He had a spectacle case in his hand, which he turned
over and over while he was thus in question, with a
certain free use of the thumb which is never seen but in a
hand accustomed to tools.

Charles Dickens, *Little Dorrit* (1855–7)

No public business of any kind could possibly be done at any time
without the acquiescence of the Circumlocution Office. Its finger was in
the largest public pie and in the smallest public tart.

Charles Dickens, *Little Dorrit* (1855–7)

It's 'ARD to GO WRONG in the SUBURBS

Verses by KAY GRANT
Illustrations by Jean Cullen

He flourished his tool. The end of the lash just touched my forehead. A warm, excited thrill ran through my veins, my blood seemed to give a bound, and then raced fast and hot along its channels. I got up nimbly, came round to where he stood, and faced him.

Charlotte Brontë, *The Professor* (1857)

I have a great respect for Miss Tompkinson; but I do assure you, sir, I'd as soon marry one of Her Majesty's Life Guards. I would rather; it would be more suitable.

Elizabeth Gaskell, *Mr Harrison's Confession* (1856)

And when you had found him, you found a man superficially coy perhaps, but at bottom always ready to do business.

Charles Reade, *It's Never Too Late to Mend* (1856)

What'er is done in this sweet isle,
There's none that may not lift his horn,
If only lifted with a smile.

William Johnson Cory, *Ionica, Poems* (1858)

A boy's sheepishness is by no means a sign of over-mastering reverence; and while you are making encouraging advances to him under the idea that he is overwhelmed by a sense of your age and wisdom, ten to one he is thinking you extremely queer.

George Elliot (Mary Ann Evans), *The Mill on the Floss* (1860)

Mrs Glegg had doubtless the glossiest and crispest brown curls in her drawers, as well as curls in various degrees of fuzzy laxness.

George Eliot, *The Mill on the Floss* (1860)

I had cherished a profound conviction that her bringing me up by hand gave her no right to bring me up by jerks.

Charles Dickens, *Great Expectations* (1860–61)

Mrs Ray declared that she had not found it at all hard and then — with laudable curiosity, seeing how little she had known about balls — desired to have an immediate account of Rachel's doings.

Anthony Trollope, *Rachel Ray* (1861)

He had an unbounded enthusiasm for French letters. He lost his sense of proportion in that matter.

George Meredith, *Modern Love* (1862)

I am not going to offer — still less urge — marriage now. But I insist on free intercourse — face to face.

John Ruskin, *Sesame and Lilies* (1864–9)

I like my balls very well and have also received the money.

William Hazlitt, *Memoirs* (1867)

A young Irish girl, going from Albany to New York to a situation, lost
     her written recommendation. Having an old friend in the city, she
     appealed to him to help her. The following is a copy of his certificate.
'This is to certify that Bridget Mahony had a good character when she
           left Albany, but lost it on the steamboat going down.'

Anonymous, *The Book of Blunders* (1871)

As big as any man could wish to
have, and lined inside, and
doubled-lined in the lower parts,
and extra piece of stiffening at
the bottom.

Thomas Hardy, *Under The Greenwood Tree* (1872)

Never travel a long journey without having your
drawers lined smoothly and carefully with chamois
leather or buckskin.

John Spencer, *Bicycling – A Book for Early Riders* (1874)

'Oh, I can't explain!' cried Roderick impatiently, returning to his work.
'I've only one way of expressing my deepest feelings – it's this.' And he
                                                    swung his tool.

Henry James, *Roderick Hudson* (1875)

'This here's a Bramah pick-lock, sir,' says Critchett,
          displaying an elegant little tool.

Ouida (Louise Ramé), *An Altruist* (1875)

'You think me a queer fellow
already. It's not easy, either, to tell
you what I feel. Not easy at all for
so queer a fellow as I tell you in how
many ways he's queer.'

Henry James, A Passionate Pilgrim (1875)

*No woman was happier in her choice — no woman —
and after two months of uninterrupted intercourse, there
is still more cause for thankfulness.*

Elizabeth Barrett Browning, Letters (1876)

'It's just like Longueville, you know,' Gordon Wright went on; 'he
always comes at you from behind; he's so awfully fond of surprises.'

Henry James, Confidence (1880)

*She gave a little scream and a jerk, and so
relieved herself.*

Anthony Trollope, The Duke's Children (1880)

*She realised at last that she had no vocation for
struggling with her combinations.*

Henry James, The Portrait of a Lady (1881)

*Gradually, when he found his sensitive organ grateful
even for grim favours, he conferred them with a lighter
hand.*

Henry James, The Portrait of a Lady (1881)

'Well, now, you look here, that was a good lay of yours last night. I don't deny it was a good lay. Some of you pretty handy with a hand-spike end.'

Robert Louis Stevenson, *Treasure Island* (1883)

Prince of the school, he had gained an easy domination over the old Greek master by the fascination of his parts.

Walter Pater, *Marius the Epicurean* (1885)

'My boy!' he said – and, if you'll believe it, his very voice was queer, almost shaky and a little broken and hoarse, not at all what you would expect an earl's voice to be, though he spoke more decidedly and peremptorily even than before – 'yes, you'll be my boy as long as I live; and, by George, sometimes I feel as if you were the only boy I ever had.'

Frances Hodgson Burnett, *Little Lord Fauntleroy* (1886)

Now the time was coming when I began to think about helping the princes by fetching their balls up from the bottom.

John Ruskin, *Praeterita* (1886-8)

It was the constant theme of his French friends. They believed that at bottom he was sorer than they were. They, however, were perpetually in the breach.

Henry James, *The Princess Casamassima* (1886)

What he heard was the tear of the ripping tool as it ploughed its way along the sticky parting.

Thomas Hardy, *The Woodlanders* (1887)

This time I left the excuses to his
more practised patience, only
relieving myself in response to a
direct appeal from a young lady
with whom, in the hall, I found
myself sitting.

Henry James, *The Reverberator* (1888)

The only thing I can think about now is being hard up.
I suppose having my hands in my pockets has made me
think of this.

Jerome K Jerome, *The Idle Thoughts of an Idle Fellow* (1889)

Her beauty smoothed earth's furrowed face!
    She gave me tokens three:
A look, a word of her winsome mouth,
    And a wild raspberry.

Francis Thompson, *Sister Songs* (1895)

Ere the wholesome flesh decay,
    And the will nerve be numb,
And the lips lack breath to say,
    'No, my lad, I cannot come.'

A E Housman, *A Shropshire Lad* (1896)

Mr Longdon, resisting, kept erect with a low gasp that his host only was
near enough to catch. This suddenly appeared to confirm an impression
gathered by Vanderbank in their contact, a strange sense that his visitor
was so agitated as to be trembling in every limb. It brought to his lips a
kind of ejaculation.

Henry James, *The Awkward Age* (1899)

What an intimacy, what an intensity of relation, I said to myself, so successful a process implied! It was, of course, familiar enough that when people were so deeply in love they rubbed off on each other.

Henry James, *The Sacred Fount* (1900)

Some great men owe most of their greatness to the ability of detecting in those they destine for their tools the exact quality of strength that matters for their work.

Joseph Conrad, *Lord Jim* (1900)

Then she had had her equal consciousness that, within five minutes, something between them had — well, she couldn't call it anything but come.

Henry James, *The Wings of the Dove* (1902)

I had done Miss Churm at the piano before — it was an attitude in which she knew how to take on an absolutely poetic grace.

Henry James, *The Real Thing* (1903)

I was nearly a man now; I would be afraid of things no more; I would get out my pendulum and see whether that would not help me. The pendulum should wag and have a fair chance of doing its best.

George MacDonald, *Wilfred Cumbermede* (1904)

'Stop a minute; let those two people go on, or I shall have to speak to them. I do detest conventional intercourse. Nasty! They are going into the church, too. Oh, the Britisher abroad!'

E M Forster, *A Room with a View* (1908)

Next after that slow-coming, slow-going smile of her lover, it was the rusty complexion of his patrimonial marbles that she most prized.

Henry James, *The Last of the Valerii* (1909)

Go, spend your penny, Beauty, when you will,
In the grave's darkness let the stamp be lost.
The water still will bubble.

John Masefield, *Lollingdon Downs* (1910)

He reached his room to find three other boys busily engaged in abusing their housemaster.

Horace Annesley Vachell, *The Hill* (1914)

'Well!' said the Duchess to me,
'apart from your balls, can't I be of
any use to you?'

Marcel Proust, *Cities of the Plain* (1921)

And when you'd a mind to career
Off anywhere – say to town –
You were all of a sudden gone
Before I had thought thereon,
Or noticed your trunks were down.

Thomas Hardy, *Without Ceremony* (1922)

Having for years had no real intercourse with any one save his wife, he was very shy.

Dame Ethel Smyth, *Impressions that Remain* (1922)

Country ladies are not like London ones, who can take a dinner, an opera, two balls and an at-home in one and the same night.

Robert Surtees, *Ask Mamma* (1924)

Eustace came too and knelt quietly enough between his aunts. But when it was over he at once got up and began hunting for something.

'Why! Someone has cut my whistle in two,' he said.

E M Forster, *The Story of a Panic* (1928)

'Hang your theories!' said Parker.
'It looks to me as if we shall have
to wash out the idea that General
Fentiman got his dose in
Portman Square.'

Dorothy L Sayers, *The Unpleasantness at the Bellona Club* (1928)

Here is a wonderful and delightful thing, that we should have furnished ourselves with orifices, with traps that open and shut, through which to push and pour alien objects that give us such pleasurable, such delicious sensations.

Rose Macaulay, *Personal Pleasures* (1935)

What is more beautiful for the blonde to wear for formal dances than white tulle? My answer — and I'm sure you will agree with me — is 'Nothing.'

Barbara Cartland, *Etiquette* (1952)

Mind you, I never made advances to a woman who wouldn't have gladly acknowledged to thirty-five. And I gave them love. Why, many of them had never known what it was to have a man do them up behind.

W Somerset Maugham, *The Round Dozen* (1953)

Mr Grant, really quite glad of an
excuse to dismount, offered his cock
to Lydia, who immediately flung
a leg over it, explaining that she
had put on a frock with pleats
on purpose.

Angela Thirkell, *The Brandons* (1953)

But I remember more dearly autumn afternoons
in bottoms that lay intensely silent under old and
great trees.

C S Lewis, *Surprised by Joy* (1955)

The chief purpose of Mrs Roosevelt in coming to London was to have
intercourse with the American troops.

Gilbert Harding, *Along My Line* (1956)

'I should like balls infinitely better,' said Caroline
Bingley, 'if they were carried in a different manner.'

C S Lewis, *Undeceptions* (1971)

She continued to argue for the
truth until gunpowder and faggots
consumed her.

Pauline Nadir, *The King's Ladies* (2000)

Deidra had quite phenomenal nipples. They were huge
and dark brown, and when aroused startlingly erect.
Men flipped over her nipples.

Jackie Collins, *Hollywood Wives – The New Generation* (2003)

Four

Sods I Have Cut on the Turf

A Library of Weird Titles

In the early sixties I left journalism when I was offered a job in publishing – working in the book business had always been one of my ambitions. I spent the next decade as an editor and ultimately editorial director of a publishing house whose list ranged from new editions of the classics to novels by major popular authors including Harold Robbins, Stephen King and James Herbert, and paperback originals geared to the latest fad or media phenomenon. These were the years of the permissive society, the Beatles and the start of the punk culture. They were also the years when the titles and cover designs of books, especially paperbacks, became a source of great competition among publishers.

Of course, titles had been important for many years and as well as those whose directness or evocative impact had made them successful there had also been a quite considerable number notable for their novelty, curiosity value and even downright strangeness. I remember as a youngster at home being amused by one title on the family bookshelf, *My Poor Dick*, which contained a bookplate stating that it had been a school prize awarded to my grandfather in 1888 for 'Composition'. It was not just the suggestiveness of the title that made me snigger in the way adolescents do, but also the author's name, John Strange Winter. In fact, it was not until many years later when I was researching Victorian authors that I discovered that Winter was actually a woman, Henrietta Vaughan Stannard, and that 'he' had published several other novels for young readers, all with equally strange titles, including *He Went for a Soldier* (1890), *A Gay Little Woman* (1897) and what I assume was another adventure of the hero of that original novel, *Dick the Faithful* (1905).

Creating titles was one of my jobs as an editor and I have mixed memories of meetings with my colleagues as we brainstormed for suitable eye-catching titles. One particular manuscript sticks in my mind. It was about a ruthless business-man who pulled off big deals with the same élan with which he pulled beautiful women. The author, Victor Briggs, and I debated for some time over a title. *Get It While You Can* seemed a bit dated in the era of *Lolita* and *Candy*, while *The Chairman's Way* was only suggestive of a business manual. In the end, we came up with a title that everyone was happy with – *Never Make Love to a Woman with Big Hands*. (Think about it!)

Some of the other gems from this period that I remember – though they were *not* my responsibility – include a thriller, *She Vamped A Strangler* by Henri Duval; a collection of risqué ballads from Australia, *It's 'Ard to Go Wrong in the Suburbs* by Kay Grant; and my particular favourite, *Sods I Have Cut on the Turf* by Jack Leach. The author was a forerunner of Dick Francis and wrote about horse racing – though you would probably not have guessed it without seeing the cover of the book. Interestingly, I read recently that the British author Simon Brett chose a not-dissimilar title for a book for younger readers, *How To Be A Little Sod*. When this was subsequently made into a television series, he was greeted, whenever he rang the production team, with the words, 'Sod Office!'

This, though, is just a handful of the titles plus straplines from among the hundreds that I discovered during publishing trips to America and Europe as well as research in the British Library, the New York Public Library and the Library of Congress in Washington, DC, not forgetting the libraries of other book collectors. Here, then, is my library of weird and wonderful books – many of them with titles almost too bad to be true, but with a guarantee that every one is absolutely genuine.

Basement Gang, David Williams (Beacon Books, 1957)
'Kathie was a virgin until she was taken in the back passage.'

Benefits of Farting Explained, Don Fartando (Fleet Street, 1602)
'A translation from the Spanish by Obidah Fizle.'

A Big Cock and a Leaking Mouth, Cheng Hsie (Shanghai publishing Co, 1964)
'It is a bad habit for children to have a meal walking about and dropping rice.'

The Big Problem of Small Organs, Alan T Kitley (Privately published, 1966)
'The results of ten years devising schemes for small organs.'

Blondes Prefer Gentlemen, 'Melita Noose' (Stanley Paul, 1926)
'Every girl is mistress of her own fate and can get on it is she wants to.'

Blondie Beg Your Bullet, Rick Razio (MC Publications, 1957)
'The man who makes the gangsters quake and the women quiver.'

Bowels Opened, Reverend Sibbes & Katherine Hall (Cambridge, 1642)
'A discovery of the near and dear love.'

Boy Hungry, Kate Nickerson (Carnival Books, 1960)
'The revealing story of a girl who learned about love the hard way.'

Briefs Calmly Considered, Thomas Taylor (Anthony Berkley, 1826)
'A layman's guide to the passage of the law.'

Brooklyn Moll Shoots Bedmate, Ernest McKeag (Modern Fiction, 1951)
'The scandal sheets all wanted to cover this gall.'

Camping Among Cannibals, Alfred St Johnston (Macmillan, 1883)
'The exploits of an explorer among savages who eat human flesh.'

Confessions of a Groper, Samu Yamamoto (Chikan Press, 1997)
'Gradually you discover the most amazing thing — no one stops you.'

Couplings up the Khyber, Percy Berridge (David & Charles, 1969)
'Railway stories from a far-flung corner.'

Crick Bottom, Ellsworthy Conkle (Samuel French, 1928)
'Another lively entertainment about a small country seat.'

Cult of the Clitoris, Noel Pemberton-Billing (Vigilante Publishing Co, 1918)
'An exaggerated clitoris might drive a woman to a bull elephant.'

Dames Fry Too, Dick Hudsen (Gannet Press Ltd, 1954)
'Things would only get hotter when she tangled with the Private Dick.'

Dumps, Mrs E T Meade (Chambers, 1905)
'The story of a plain girl and her struggles in life.'

Dykes on Bikes, Alan Marshall (Lion Books, 1973)
'There was no hell on earth like these girls!'

Every Frenchman Has One, Olivia De Havilland. (Paul Elek, 1963)
'The intimate revelations of a great Hollywood film star!'

Fables of Abundance, Jackson Lears (Hollywood House, 1974)
'The dream of glimpsing half-dressed women unawares!'

Farting Candles, Lillian Sayce (Skeffington, 1935)
'A masterpiece of pungent brevity about the scandalous ladies of Upwitham.'

Fifty Years with the Rod, John Stirling (Philip Allan, 1929)
'A lifetime of great catches by the President of the Scottish Anglers' Association.'

Fountain of Youth, Dr. Benedict Lust (Macfadden Publications, 1923)
'Contains full details of Dr Lust's Technique of Rectal Irrigation.'

Franny Dill, Woodrow Olivetti (Triumph Books, 1967)
'The scorching saga of a teenage sex-bomb.'

The Future of Nakedness, John Langdon-Davies (Noel Douglas, 1929)
'A revealing look at where our obsession with clothes is leading.'

Garden of Ignorance, Mrs Marion Cran (Herbert Jenkins Ltd, 1930)
'The experiences of a woman in a garden by the author of Story of My Ruin.'

Gay Boys of Old Yale, John Denison Vose (Hunter Books, 1869)
'Carefree varsity days recalled by one of them.'

Gay Crusaders, Magdalen King-Hall (Peter Davis, 1934)
'A stirring romance of men of action in the Middle Ages.'

Glad to be Bad, Adam Roberts (Midwood, 1977)
'Gorgeous Gwen was always willing to give a little to get a lot.'

Grand Opening, Alice Leeds (Thomas Nelson, 1980)
'A year in the life of a total wife.'

Green Balls, Paul Bewsher (Blackwood & Sons, 1919)
'The dramatic adventures of a Night Bomber.'

Groping, Naomi Jacob (Hutchinson, 1933)
'The intimate story of Marcus Stern's struggle against adversity.'

Half-Cocked, Violet Grey (Command Books, 1975)
'He was hard up and horny all the time but only half a man.'

Her Candle Burns Hot, Hodge Evans (Rainbow Books, 1970)
'On her wedding night a strange man walked in . . .'

History of Fanny Thoughtless, Anonymous (J Davis, 1825)
'What befell naughty Fanny when she would not learn her lesson.'

Hookers of Kew, Mea Allan (Michael Joseph, 1967)
'A revealing biography of the eminent family of botanists.'

How to Avoid Intercourse with your Unfriendly Car Mechanic, Harold M Landy (Ashley Books, 1977)
'A guide to getting the best servicing.'

Invisible Dick, Frank Topham (D C Thompson, 1936)
'"What a disgraceful scene," said Dick Brett, doing a series of physical jerks behind a bush.'

Joyful Lays, Richard Lowry & Howard Doane (Biglow & Main, 1886)
'Words and music for rousing passion in worship.'

Leadership Secrets of Attila the Hun, Wess Roberts (Bantam Press, 1989)
'Good Huns normally achieve what their chieftain expects of them.'

Lesbia's Little Blunder, Bessie Marchant (Frederick Warne, 1934)
'Lesbia has to learn that love wins the affection of her school chums.'

Life, Love and Meatloaf, Mike Randall (Brandon House, 1964)
'A cookbook for bachelors.'

Living with Crazy Buttocks, Kaz Cooke (Penguin, 2002)
'Another comic milestone by the author of Real Gorgeous.'

Love Slave of the Scientists, Frank Belknap Long (Avon Books, 1953)
'When the scientists invented these delectable toys they reckoned without the unstable passions of wives.'

Love Sonnets of a Hoodlum, Wallace Irwin (Paul Elder & Co, 1901)
'The vagaries of a man of the world.'

Loves of a Girl Wrestler, Ben West (Beacon Books, 1969)
'A Terror in the Ring . . . A Tigress in the Boudoir.'

Making It in Leather, Vincent Hayes (Drake Publishers, 1972)
'The secrets of beautiful designs for family and friends.'

A Man, a Maid and Saturn's Temptation, Stanley G Weinbaum (Avon Books, 1953)
'Diana Vick had his jealously sought jewels in her hand and a morass ahead.'

Manual of Lies, Bartholomew Inganerole (*c.* sixteenth century)
'Methods for wrongdoing: adultery before a wife and lust before a maiden, including the counterfeiting of virginity and crafty means for the bedding of a shy maid.'

Memorable Balls, James Laver (Derek Verschoyle, 1954)
'An eminent historian's study of some great social entertainments.'

Naked on Roller Skates, Maxwell Bodenheim (Monarch Books 1954)
'Bump and grind was their idea of fun.'

Nautipuss, Clyde Allison (Ember Library, 1985)
'Agent 0008 Battles the Temptress of the Deep.'

Penetrating Wagner's Ring, John Di Gaetanao (De Capo Press, 1978
'A musician's in-depth examination of the great composer's most famous creation.'

Perfect 36, Ed Springarn (Pyramid Books, 1973)
'A revealing story of the bosom business.'

Perverse Pussy, Anonymous (American Sunday-School Union 1869)
'The story of raising a difficult cat – and the lessons to be drawn.'

Pit Stop Nympho, Peter Kevin (Imperial Books, 1978)
'Into the high tension world of Grand Prix racing roars red-hot lust!'

Planet of the Knob Heads, Stanton A Coblentz (Blue Ribbon, 1939
'It was a race against time to save the women from their deadly embrace.'

Queer Shipmates, Archibald Campbell (Phoenix House, 1962)
'Afloat on the oceans of the world with some unusual seamen.'

Queer Sisters, Steve Harragani (Stallion Books, 1963)
'A penetrating story of Society's Greatest Curse: Homosexuality!'

Quickie!, Gerald Foster (Quarter Books, 1974)
'She was always one jump ahead of the mobsters.'

Resistance of Piles to Penetration, Russell V Allin (Spon, 1935)
'Essential study for all those engaged in the building industry.'

Romantic Shorts, Mollie Panter-Downes (Swan, 1941)
'Audrey was left breathless by the fervour of his love-making.'

Saddle of Queens, Louise Bloodgood (J A Allen, 1959)
'Some of the great historical rides of royalty.'

Sauciest Boy in the Service, W Gordon Stables (Ward Lock, 1905)
'A story of pluck and perseverance among staunch military men.'

Scouts in Bondage, Geoffrey Prout (Aldine Publishing Co, 1930)
'Helpful hints for Boy Scouts to lead more adventurous lives.'

She Vamped a Strangler, Henri Duval (Murray & Nichols, 1948)
'Why can't young girls realise it's madly dangerous to vamp most men!'

A Short History of Fingers, H Allen Smith (Little Brown, 1963)
'Never stick your finger in a woman's business.'

Sorority Sluts, Jan Hudson (Midwood, 1962)
'It was a lushly curved nymph of a teacher who taught him the real lessons.'

A Stress Analysis of the Strapless Evening Gown, Francis O Chisholm (Prentice-Hall, 1963)
'When things are going well, something will go wrong and let you down.'

A Study of Masturbation, John Francis Meagher (Bailliere, Tindall & Cox, 1924)
'Any recommendation to marry in order to cure this habit is abominably unfair.'

Suggestive Thoughts for Busy Workers, Osborne Keen (Christian Book Room, 1883)
'Uplifting ideas for men and women to practise daily.'

She Vamped a Strangler

by HENRI DUVAL

COMPLETE
9D
NOVEL

KAY

Crime and Passion Series

Syphilis: or A Poetical History of the French Disease, Nahum Tate (London, 1686)
'So delicately revealed it may be read by the purest maidens.'

Tomcats in Tights, Jack Hanley (Avon Books, 1955)
'They were two pussies who really knew how to come on in Broadway.'

Tosser, Gunman, Frank Carr (Ward Lock, 1939)
'Betty's fingers gripped her quirt tightly; she, too, had heard of Tosser Smith.'

Twilight Girls: Down with Men!, Judson Grey (Epic Originals, 1962)
'The lascivious, lady-lusting League of Amazons.'

Under Two Queens, John Skrine (Macmillan, 1884)
'His life was dedicated to the service of two great beauties.'

Ups and Downs of Lady Di, Annette Lyster (Brentano's, 1907)
'She little knew a handsome prince would seal her fate.'

Warped Women, Jane Pritchard (Lion Books, 1962)
'Strange love stripped them of all decency.'

What's Wrong with Bottoms?, P Hessell & J Nelson (Hutchinson, 1987)
'An amusing book for children with lots of coloured illustrations.'

Women on the Job, Judith Buber Agassi (Lexington Books, 1979)
'A lively account of the activities of professional women.'

Women's Worth, Anonymous (London, seventeenth century)
'A treatise proving by sundry reasons that women do excel men.'

Ever since 1978, the Diagram Group has given an annual award for the Oddest Title of the Year, which began auspiciously with *Proceedings of the Second International Workshop on Nude Mice*.

Many of the titles already listed appeared too early for inclusion in this award, but in the quarter of a century since the 'accolade' was first bestowed there has been a constant stream of entries all demonstrating that around the world publishers and their editors continue to have few reservations about foisting on the reading public some truly extraordinary volumes – no doubt hoping that *someone* will buy a copy. (Publishers might like to note that one of the British Museum titles, *A List of Fragments Rejoined in the Kuyunjik Collection*, has been in stock for 90 years, selling about three copies a year.)

Here are a hundred or so of the titles entered for the Diagram award with the names of the authors omitted to spare any embarrassment they might feel.

After the Orgy: Towards a Politics of Exhaustion
Anorexia Nervosa in Bulgarian Bees
Art and Craft of Pounding Flowers
Be Bold With Bananas
Big Book of Lesbian Horse Stories
Career Management in House Prostitution
Chicken Little Jane on the Big John
Children Are Like Wet Cement
Common Teasel as a Carnivorous Plant
Constipation and our Civilisation
Cooking with God
Do-it-Yourself Lobotomy
Eat Your House
Enjoy Your Chameleon
Entertaining with Insects
Explosive Spiders and How to Make Them
Explorations at Sodom
Fashion Is Spinach
Fish Who Answer the Telephone
Flat-Footed Flies of Europe
Flying Without a Broom
Follow Your Broken Nose

Frog Raising for Pleasure and Profit
Games You Can Play with Your Pussy
Gentle Art of Cooking Wives
Great Pantyhose Craft Book
Greek Rural Postmen and their Cancellation Numbers
Hand Grenade Throwing as a College Sport
Have Fun with Rats
Healing Sounds of the Didgeridoo
Highlights in the History of Concrete
History and Romance of Elastic Webbing
Hot Topics in Urology
How to Become a Schizophrenic
How to be Happy though Married
How to Cook Husbands
How to Pick Pockets
I Can Taste and Smell
Jaws and Teeth of Ancient Hawaiians
Jilling Off: Women's Masturbation Stories
Joy of Chickens
Joy of the Upright Man
Keep Warm with an Axe
Keeping Your Tools Tiptop
Knitting in the Fast Lane
Lightweight Sandwich Construction
Manhole Covers of Los Angeles
Melons for the Passionate Grower
Money-Laundering Training Manual
My Invisible Friend Explains the Bible
Nasal Maintenance: Nursing Your Nose
New Guinea Tapeworms and Jewish Grandmothers
One Hour Orgasm
One Hundred Years of British Catering
Optical Chick Sexing
Oral Sadism and the Vegetarian Personality
Our Lady of the Potatoes
Passing Gas

Penis Sheaths and their Distribution in Africa
Personality of Meat
Phone Calls from the Dead
Play with Your Own Marbles
Post-Mortem Collectibles
Practical Embalmer
Practical Guide for Inspectors of Nuisances
Pranks with the Mouth
Psoriasis at Your Fingertips
Queer Doings in the Navy
Recollections of Squatting in Victoria
Red-Haired Irish Women on the Bog
Reusing Old Graves
Romance of Leprosy
Safe Sex in the Garden
Scurvy Past and Present
Second-Hand Parrots: A Complete Owner's Pet Manual
Secrets Your Snake Wants You to Know
Sex After Death
Sex Instruction for Irish Farmers
Simply Bursting: A Story of Bladder Control
Smelling: My Story
Social History of the Machine Gun
Sociological History of Excretory Experience
Some Accounts of the Beard and the Moustache
Stop Cocks in the Liver Building, 1912
Straight Talk About Surgical Penis Enlargement
Straight to Hell: Great Suicides of the Twentieth Century
Tasty Dishes from Waste Items
Tea Bag Folding
Teach Yourself Alcoholism
Theory of Lengthwise Rolling
Three Weeks in Wet Sheets
Toddler's Guide to the Rubber Industry
Truncheons – Their Romance and Reality
Truss Fun

Views of Gentlemen's Seats
Weeds in a Changing World
Who's Who in Barbed Wire
Who's Who in Cocker Spaniels
Whose Bottom is This? A Lift-the-Flap Book
Why Bring This Up? A Guide to Seasickness
Wigglers, Undulators and their Application
Without Regret: A Handbook for Owners of Canine Amputees
Women and Integrated Pest Management
Wood Carving with a Chainsaw
Your Friend, the Computer Hacker

The Literary Laboratory

What's That Noshin' on My Leg?

A Grab-Bag of Discarded Titles

It was, I think, the writer and broadcaster, Ludovic Kennedy, who told one of the most amusing stories about titling books. It concerned J M Barrie, the author of *Peter Pan*, who throughout his life helped a number of aspiring writers, including one who was having a particular problem finding a title for his manuscript. According to Kennedy, Barrie asked the young man, 'Are there any horses in the story?' When he was told there were none, he enquired, 'And are there any trumpets in it?' Again the now somewhat bemused writer shook his head, at which Barrie replied, 'Well, why not call it *No Horses or Trumpets?*'

Whether the great man was just being facetious, there is now no way of telling. But I do know from my own years in publishing – and from an even longer period of time as an author – that getting the title right can be a tortuous business. Over the years there have certainly been many books that have suffered from an improbable title, while just as many have benefited from a good one. In this context I am reminded of a story about one of my favourite horror novels, *Dr Jekyll and Mr Hyde*, told by the author himself, Robert Louis Stevenson, a man known to enjoy a play on words. While giving an interview in New York in 1887, Stevenson told a reporter who was mispronouncing the title that the name Jekyll should be pronounced with an initial long 'e' as in 'Geekill' but not as in 'Dzeckle' or 'Jeckel'. As Stevenson knew French, this suggests that the surname was intended to signify '*Je* kill' meaning '*I* kill' and hence the title of the novel had a special significance and could be read as 'I Kill and Hide'.

Ernest Hemingway was one author we know devoted a lot of time to the titles of his stories and books – but did not give thought to them until after he had finished the work in progress. 'Sometimes I have as many as a hundred,' he was once quoted, 'then I start eliminating them – sometimes all of them.' Raymond Chandler was also always seeking the perfect title and kept a little notebook in which he jotted down any ideas that came to him. After his death, the book was found to contain dozens of wonderful titles that he never used, including *The Man with the Shredded Ear, Lament But No Tears* and *The Corpse Came in Person.* Perhaps, though, no writer was stranger in his choice than the poet e e cummings who called one book *No Thanks,* a second *CIOPW* – short for charcoal, ink, oils, pencil and watercolour – and in 1930 published a book with no title at all! Below is a selection of some titles that *might* have adorned now very famous books, but were mercifully confined to oblivion before the presses rolled.

1813

First Impressions by Jane Austen

The rector's daughter, whose writing ranged from a satire on the Gothic fiction of her time to penetrating studies of human behaviour, had trouble finding the right title for one of the most enduring of all her books – until finally settling on the all-encompassing . . . *Pride and Prejudice.*

1818

Prometheus Unchained by Mary Shelley

The daughter of the feminist pioneer, Mary Wollstonecraft, Mary Shelley eloped with the poet Percy Shelley when she was still in her teens. While the pair were in Switzerland she wrote the novel about a scientist's creation of a man-made being, which could have appeared under this title until the inspired choice of her husband to call it . . . *Frankenstein*.

1844

Martin Sweetlewag by Charles Dickens

The great novelist was one of the most prolific creators of alternative titles for his stories, many of which were originally published as serials in magazines. This creativity was particularly furious after a visit to America in 1842 with the story that he called – apart from the above – *Martin Sweetledew*, then *Martin Chuzzletow* before deciding on . . . *Martin Chuzzlewit*.

1848

The Novel Without a Hero by William Thackeray

Born in Calcutta, Thackeray dissipated his inheritance while still a young man, turned to journalism to make his way, and after a series of works under various pseudonyms – including Fitzbootle, Titmarsh and Snob – began the series of novels that made his name. His tale of a social climber making her way through the decadent upper classes of London was almost on the verge of being published when Thackeray had second thoughts – and suggested . . . *Vanity Fair*.

1853

Tom-All-Alone's Factory That Got into Chancery and Never Got Out by Charles Dickens

A mystery story of forgery, blackmail and murder that introduced Inspector Bucket, the first significant detective in English literature, provided Dickens with a similar headache when it came to a title and apart from this long-winded version, he also considered *The Ruined House* and *The East Wind* before deciding on the simple . . . *Bleak House*.

1854

Two and Two Are Four by Charles Dickens

The evidence of a letter to his editor reveals that Dickens lavished even more possible titles on his next serial of unrelenting human misery, including *A Mere Question of Figures*, *Hard Heads and Soft Hearts*, *Prove It*, *Rust and Dust*, *Hard-Headed Gradgrind*, *According to Cocker* and – appropriately – *Stubborn Things*, until, finally, the solution was found in . . . *Hard Times*.

1857

Les Limbs by Charles Baudelaire

This was the French poet's original title for his group of macabre poems intended as an acknowledgment to the Limbo described in Dante Alighieri's *Divina Commedia*, until it changed following a suggestion by the critic Hippolyte Babou that it would sound better as . . . *Les Fleurs du Mal*.

1860

St. Ogg's on the Floss by George Eliot

Mary Ann Evans, who published her novels under the pseudonym 'George Eliot', discussed several alternative titles for her story of rural morality including this one, *Sister Maggie* and *The House of Tulliver* before finally accepting her publisher's suggestion – *The Mill on the Floss*.

1864

All's Well That Ends Well by Leo Tolstoy

The famous Russian novelist, philosopher and mystic lead a dissolute life at university and on the family farm until he joined the army. Tolstoy's experiences in the Crimean War deeply affected him and a series of sketches and tales about the horrors of battle culminated in a book described as one of the greatest novels ever written. The author's initial title was *1825*, but when he abandoned any thoughts of a happy ending, he settled for the unsurpassable: *War and Peace*.

1880

Judah: A Tale of the Christ by Lew Wallace

Wallace, a soldier from Indiana who became the governor of Utah in 1878, spent years writing his novel about the violent birth of Christianity. Just before the book was published, it was suggested to him that a simpler title with more impact and sales appeal would be . . . *Ben-Hur*.

1883

The Sea-Cook by Robert Louis Stevenson

The Scottish-born author, who briefly trained to follow his family profession as an engineer, instead travelled and made his name with essays and tales based on his experiences in Europe and America. His fame was assured by the high adventure tale about a search for a pirate's buried loot that he was advised to retitle . . . *Treasure Island*.

1891

The Body and Soul of Sue by Thomas Hardy

An architect turned writer, Hardy brilliantly portrayed both the underside of rural life and its idylls in his series of Wessex novels. The powerful story of one of his doomed heroines went through several other titles including *Too Late, Beloved* and *Tess of the Hardys* before appearing as . . . *Tess of the D'Urbervilles*.

1895

Private Fleming, His Various Battles by Stephen Crane

The American writer and war correspondent, who switched from writing stories of urban life to tales set on the battlefield, made a last-minute decision to alter the title of his Civil War epic and came up with – *The Red Badge of Courage*.

1896

The Recalcitrants by Thomas Hardy

Hardy again considered several titles when he completed his explicit novel about a man made an outcast because of his shocking behaviour. Initially called *The Simpleton*, it went through *The Recalcitrants* to *Hearts Insurgent,* before finally reaching the presses as . . . *Jude the Obscure.*

1897

The Un-Dead by Bram Stoker

Irish-born Abraham Stoker worked as a clerk and then for many years as manager to the actor Sir Henry Irving, only having time for his writing when off duty. Without even visiting the setting of his story about a vampire count in Transylvania, he created arguably the most famous horror novel of all – making a rapid title change just before the manuscript was to be printed to the immortal . . . *Dracula.*

1903

Ernest Pontifex by Samuel Butler

The English author, painter and musician famous during his lifetime for his Utopian satire, *Erewhon* (1872) – the title is an inversion of 'nowhere' – did not live to see the publication of his final novel about four generations of an ill-starred family earn him a place in literary history after a title change to . . . *The Way of All Flesh.*

1905

From a Sense of Duty by E M Forster

The academic Forster became famous for his stories of English middle-class life during the first decade of the century with their special insight into public schools, the Church and the civil service. His first novel, set in Italy, was submitted as a serial under the title, *Monteriano,* renamed *From a Sense of Duty,* but it was ultimately published as . . . *Where Angels Fear to Tread.*

1915

The Saddest Story by Ford Madox Ford

This English-born writer was gassed in the early months of the First World War, but survived to write several atmospheric novels about the conflict plus some fine poetry. Although his classic love story did not feature the war at all, the title was deliberately changed to sound more patriotic in war-torn Britain: *The Good Soldier*.

Beauty and Ashes by W Somerset Maugham

The English writer Maugham served with a Red Cross unit in France in 1914 and then as a secret agent before coming to public attention with a largely autobiographical tragedy that he had some difficulty in entitling. After abandoning his first idea he decided upon – *Of Human Bondage*.

1920

The Village Virus by Sinclair Lewis

The son of a doctor, Lewis became a journalist and made his reputation with books exposing the intolerance and materialism of American society that began with this story of hypocrisy in a small community. On publication, the retitled book was widely condemned, but still gave a new expression to the language . . . *Main Street*.

1925

Trimalchio in West Egg by F Scott Fitzgerald

Fitzgerald, who would become labelled as the chronicler of the 'Jazz Age', had problems with the titles of several of his books, notably his tale of sex and debauchery among the super-rich on Long Island. After objections by his publishers to this title, other suggestions included *The High-bouncing Lover* and *Gold-Batted Gatsby* before the final choice was made: *The Great Gatsby*.

Four Years of Struggle Against Lies, Stupidity and Cowardice by Adolf Hitler

The extraordinary testimony of a man hell-bent on world-domination was dictated to one of his acolytes, Rudolph Hess, while the author was serving nine months' imprisonment in Landsberg Jail in Germany. The pernicious volume might even have disappeared without trace, but for the inexorable rise of its author and a title change to . . . *Mein Kampf* (*My Struggle*).

Griffiths by Theodore Dreiser

An American journalist who worked in Chicago, St Louis and New York, Dreiser's first, starkly realistic novel *Sister Carrie* (1900) was criticised for obscenity, but his story of the weak-willed murderer Griffiths became an international success when it was retitled . . . *An American Tragedy*.

1928

John Thomas and Lady Jane by D H Lawrence

The son of a miner, this great English novelist, who achieved success with his first novel, *The White Peacock* (1911), laboured over the titles of most of his books. His classic tale of illicit love between the classes, later prosecuted for obscenity, had its title changed from the original to . . . *Lady Chatterley's Lover*.

1929

Poisonville by Dashiell Hammett

The 'founding father' of American hard-boiled fiction, Hammett worked as a successful private detective before turning his attention to writing, and establishing himself as one of the great crime story writers. His first story of the nameless 'Continental Op' went through several other title changes including *Murder Plus*, *The City of Death*, *The Wilsson Matter*, until finally it became – *Red Harvest*.

They Are Strange and They Are Lost by Thomas Wolfe

Born in North Carolina, Wolfe was to write some of the most minutely realistic but at the same time lyrical novels of the first half of the twentieth century, often drawn from his own experiences. His first novel was based very much on his youth and his initial title summarised his feelings: *O Lost*. After the above title had also been rejected, Wolfe suggested *The Exile's Story* and *The Lost Language*, only to have his publisher provide the solution: *Look Homeward, Angel*.

1933

Wives of Geniuses I Have Sat With by Gertrude Stein

This American writer whose salon and patronage of the arts in Paris in the early years of the twentieth century was hugely influential on many writers, always had trouble with her titles, especially with her autobiographical works. The title destined to ensure Stein's reputation – featuring her lifelong companion whose notorious cookbook contained a recipe for 'Hashish Brownies' – veered from *My Life with the Great* to *My 25 Years with Gertrude Stein* to the enduring . . . *The Autobiography of Alice B. Toklas*.

1934

Bar B-Q by James M Cain

A newspaperman and political columnist until the 1930s, Cain then wrote what would make him a legend in crime fiction. The novel about a young drifter and his attraction for the sexy wife of a rural café owner, which results in the pair plotting to murder the old man, was finally issued as . . . *The Postman Always Rings Twice.*

The Infernal Grove by John O'Hara

For several decades one of the top-selling literary authors in America, O'Hara had spent years writing his first book about a young man trying to cope with a middle-class life. He was at a loss what to call the book and even when he found the title that would help make his reputation, there were still many others who remained unconvinced because of its exotic connotations: *Appointment in Samara.*

1935

The Lost by Christopher Isherwood

The English novelist who became famous for stories based on his time as a tutor in the decadence of post-slump, pre-Hitler Berlin, saw his work go through title changes after his original choice. *The Lost* gave way to the more evocative, *The Last of Mr Norris*, the omnibus volume, *Berlin Tales*, and finally . . . *I Am a Camera.*

1936

Ba! Ba! Black Sheep by Margaret Mitchell

Mitchell, who was born in Atlanta, Georgia, studied medicine for a while before turning to journalism, and then spent years creating one of the most popular and influential novels of the century. The story, with its Civil War background, began life as *Pansy*, was then rapidly changed from *Milestones* to *Tote The Weary Load, Tomorrow Is Another Day* – even *Ba! Ba! Black Sheep* – before the immortal . . . *Gone With The Wind* was chosen.

Dark House by William Faulkner

After writing about his service in the First World War in his early fiction, Faulkner focused his attention on the horrors of society, in particular the harsh life in the American South. The title of this complex tale of plantation life just prior to the outbreak of the Civil War was changed by the author to a quote from the Bible: *Absalom, Absalom!*

1937

Something That Happened by John Steinbeck

An American writer revered for his realistic, compassionate novels of lowly people, Steinbeck created two unforgettable characters in this tale of the mentally retarded big man, Lennie, and his little friend, George. Unhappy with the working title, Steinbeck found the phrase that really summarised the plot in a Robert Burns poem: *Of Mice and Men*.

1940

The Mute by Carson McCullers

The American novelist McCullers, who was born in Georgia and wrote psychological tales set mainly in her native South, was encouraged to change the original title of what proved to be her masterpiece to – *The Heart is a Lonely Hunter*.

Zounds, He Dies by Raymond Chandler

The English-born master of American hard-boiled fiction changed the titles of several of his books, perhaps none more dramatically than this Philip Marlowe case inspired by Shakespeare's *Richard III*. He apparently also debated over *The Second Murderer* and *Sweet Bells Jangle*, before the choice was finally made for . . . *Farewell, My Lovely*.

1941

Three Tenant Families by James Agee

The memorable collaboration of this American writer with photographer Walker Evans highlighted the plight of poor workers in words and pictures; it was published under the evocative Biblical quote: *Let Us Now Praise Famous Men.*

1942

The Brasher Doubloon by Raymond Chandler

Chandler and his editor had several exchanges about the proposed title for another of his greatest thrillers – during which *The Brasher Doubloon* was proposed and rejected because of a fear that 'Brasher' (an ancient coin) might get pronounced as 'Brassiere'. The final vote went to . . . *The High Window.*

1945

The House of the Faith by Evelyn Waugh

The irascible English author of some of the most sardonic and entertaining books about the social life of the country from the twenties onwards might not, perhaps, have had one of his greatest successes without a title change to: *Brideshead Revisited.*

1947

Blanche's Chair in the Moon by Tennessee Williams

This American dramatist, who also wrote some fine short stories and novels, puzzled over the titles of many of his works, including his powerful erotic drama about a faded New Orleans belle. Originally entitled *The Moth*, the play was also referred to by the girl's name as well as *The Poker Night*, before its final version that won a Pulitzer Prize: *A Streetcar Named Desire.*

1949

Night Without Mercy by Nelson Algren

The Chicago-born Algren was a notable title-meddler and his gritty portrait of a drug addict and gambler was again changed to *The Neon Wilderness* before all the parties concerned were satisfied with . . . *The Man with the Golden Arm.*

The Last Man in Europe by George Orwell

Born in Bengal, Orwell served for some years in the Indian police before fighting in the Spanish Civil War and acting as a war correspondent during the Second World War – all of which inspired his later work. This title for his classic novel about a scientifically perfected servile state remained until just before publication when Orwell decided to postpone his awful prophecy by simply reversing the date he had written it: *Nineteen Eighty-Four.*

1951

If Wishes Were Horses by James Jones

The American author of two of the greatest novels of the Second World War agonised over the title for his first book about life in a heaving, unsettled army camp. This version was rejected, along with *Old Soldiers Never Die* and *They Merely Fade Away*, before Jones and his publisher agreed on – *From Here to Eternity.*

1954

Llareggub by Dylan Thomas

The Welsh-born poet and short-story writer whose lifestyle scandalised many people – though it also helped to ensure his legend – rose to international fame with a wonderful evocation of small-town Welsh life which he initially called *Quite Early One Morning*. However, his irreverent sense of humour made him change the title to that of his fictional community – read it backwards – until he was persuaded to use the more acceptable: *Under Milk Wood*.

To Climb the Wall by Evan Hunter

The former New York schoolteacher whose book was to present the first detailed story of violence in city schools might not have become an international bestseller without a title change as this version had already been used by a nun on her account of her escape from a very repressive convent! In its place was inserted the more gritty . . . *Blackboard Jungle.*

1955

The Kingdom by the Sea by Vladimir Nabokov

The hugely controversial novel by the Russian author about a middle-aged man's infatuation with a precociously experienced young girl, began its life with the heroine named Virginia and the book to be called *Ginny*. For a time she was renamed Juanita Dark, before making the final transformation into the *teenage femme fatale* – and becoming the unforgettable – *Lolita.*

1961

Catch-14 by Joseph Heller

Heller's classic American anti-war satire, which ultimately provided a famous catch phrase, actually went through two title changes before reaching the bookstalls. The author's original title was *Catch-14*. This was changed to *Catch-18* as publication neared, but then hastily retitled to avoid confusion with another forthcoming title, *Mila 18* by Leon Uris. The book finally made it with . . . *Catch-22*.

A Candle at Midnight by Sloan Wilson

Wilson was a New York reporter whose fascination with the world of big business inspired his most famous novel and also created a phrase that is now familiar all over the world. The engrossing story of men engaged in a cruel and cut-throat existence was just a few weeks away from publication when the author's wife made the observation about the city's businessmen that perfectly suited the book: *The Man in the Gray Flannel Suit*.

1956

Not Moisten an Eye by Edwin O'Connor

Irish-American O'Connor contrived to write one of the great novels about the Irish in the New World around the figure of a city mayor fighting his last political campaign. At the urging of his editor, however, the author agreed to change the folksy title to the more evocative and enduring . . . *The Last Hurrah*.

Finnerty's Ball by Nelson Algren

The second of Algren's harsh portraits of the underworld of Chicago went through a second title change to *Somebody in Boots* until the author and publisher agreed upon – *A Walk on the Wild Side*.

1962

Sex for the Single Woman by Helen Gurley Brown

This ground-breaking book by the editor of the American magazine, *Cosmopolitan*, had its title changed before going to press when Brown was told her title was rather too 'immoral'. Instead it became . . . *Sex and the Single Woman.*

1963

The Yo-Yo World of Benny Profane by Thomas Pynchon

The enigmatic American writer, whose identity has for years been the subject of much debate, broke into print with a bestseller about a man every bit as mysterious as his creator. The manuscript was entitled *Low Lands*, but was subsequently given several new versions including *World on a String, The*

Quest of Herbert Strencil, Blood's a Rover, Of a Fond Ghoul, Th
Republican Party Is a Machine and *Dream Tonight of Peacock Tails*
before the ultimate in simplicity was chosen: *V.*

1964

The Parts Nobody Knows by Ernest Hemingway

Hemingway confessed to listing dozens of possible titles for hi
books, but did not live to see the final version of his last work
This account of his life as a tyro writer in Paris in the twentie
could alternatively have been known as *It Is Different in the Ring*
The Eye and the Ear, Love Is Hunger and *To Write It Truly* – but i
was Hemingway's widow, Mary, who settled the issue with . .
A Moveable Feast.

Don't Shoot Until You See the Pupils by Bel Kaufman

The American former teacher turned novelist's comic master
piece about school life was easier to write than entitle, Kaufmar
later admitted. Once her manuscript was complete, it wen
under several names including *Hi, Teach!, The Paper World o*
Sylvia Barrett and *Please Do Not Erase* before arriving at . . . *Up th*
Down Staircase.

1968

Couples and Houses and Days by John Updike

This provocative novel with its artful insights into sex, love
marriage and adultery behind the lace curtains of suburbar
America was to make its author into an international bestselle
once he had accepted the decision of his publishers to shorter

his original title to . . . *Couples.*

They Don't Build Statues to Businessmen by Jacqueline Susann

An American journalist's sensational novel of the sex and drugs lifestyle of a group of women in the swinging sixties is another book of the period that would probably never have achieved its millions of sales without a title change to – *Valley of the Dolls.*

1969

The Birds and the Bees by David R Reuben

This revolutionary book about the latest medical and scientific discoveries to enable sexual pleasure to be more exciting, fulfilling and safer would have been published with a rather innocuous title except for a last-minute change to what is now a catch phrase: *Everything You Always Wanted to Know About Sex – But Were Afraid to Ask.*

A Jewish Patient Begins His Analysis by Philip Roth

The story of a brilliant Jewish boy and his obsession from childhood with women and sexuality was given this innocuous title by Roth to describe how the clash between his secret thoughts and morals increases as he grows up. A recommendation by the author's editor changed it before publication to the memorable: *Portnoy's Complaint.*

1972

Come and Go by Xaviera Hollander

Described as one of the books that helped to bring sex out of the closet, it told the story of the most influential madam in New York and proved a landmark in the struggle for sexual freedom. The eventual sales in excess of 16 million were undoubtedly helped by the title change to . . . *The Happy Hooker*.

Suspended Women by Gail Goodwin

The leading American novelist of such bestsellers as *The Finishing School* (1985), *A Southern Family* (1987) and *Father Melancholy's Daughter* (1991) has admited to frequently changing the titles of her books between writing and publication, a habit that began in the seventies with this tale, now known as – *Glass People*.

1974

What's That Noshin' on My Leg? by Peter Benchley

Benchley's famous novel of one man's obsessive hunt for a marine killer was given several dozen titles – including *A Silence in the Water*, *Leviathan Rising*, *Great White*, *The Shark*, even this not-altogether serious suggestion from the author's father, Nathaniel Benchley – before an unbeatable solution surfaced: *Jaws*.

At This Point in Time by Bob Woodward & Carl Bernstein

The book that brought down President Nixon described in relentless detail how the machinations of what became known as 'The Watergate Scandal' were painstakingly unearthed by two reporters on the *Washington Post*, but probably owed its ultimate success to the title change . . . to *All The President's Men*.

1977

Before This Anger by Alex Haley

Another landmark book, by a black author who traced his origins back to Africa and focused attention on the plight of his people in America. The work went through several title changes before finally being published as . . . *Roots.*

1985

Panasonic by Don DeLillo

An unsettling novel about America's consumer culture and the use of powerful advertising slogans, this book included references to many of them during the course of the narrative and DeLillo originally picked the name of the Japanese electronic giant for his title. When the company's lawyers threatened a suit for trademark infringement, a safer alternative was chosen: *White Noise.*

2003

If You Don't Have Big Breasts, Put Ribbons on Your Pigtails by Barbara Corcoran

Corcoran, a Manhattan real estate broker, drew on childhood lessons from her mother and her experiences in New York to write this celebrated self-help book about getting on in business. Ultimately, however, she acceded to the wishes of her publishers that the title might prove too provocative and changed it to . . . *Use What You've Got & Other Business Lessons I Learned.*

Tolkien is Hobbit-Forming

Literary Graffiti from the World's Walls

No book such as this could possibly exist without a chapter devoted to graffiti, the compelling art of defacement created by a secretive army of anonymous writers that might also be described as the ultimate slip of the pen. It should be no surprise that great books and authors have been the subject of many of these uniquely stylish and meaningful messages, which may be referred to in a parody of Jack London as 'The Scrawls of the Wild'. One of the earliest that sticks in my mind was to be found in the Reading Room of the British Museum, where a wag had written, 'It's a funny old world – Karl Marx.' Another favourite was inscribed in the British Library toilets, 'T S Eliot = Toilets', while a graffiti-covered wall in the Bodleian Library, Oxford, carried a more prosaic message, but one nonetheless guaranteed to raise a smile, 'This wall has been designated MS Bodl 10000 and will shortly be taken away for binding.' On a visit to the New York Public Library, I chuckled over 'Judge

Crater is Hiding Behind the Sex Books' (although I had no idea *who* the judge was) and was equally amused by another on the walls of the Sorbonne in Paris, 'We don't have time to write.'

In fact, nameless scribes have been writing these compelling messages since the time of the Roman Empire – the word graffiti derives from the Italian 'graffio' meaning 'a scratch' – and a classic example came to light in the late eighteenth century when the ruins of Pompeii were being excavated. Underneath the detritus caused by the fatal eruption of Vesuvius was found a Latin inscription that stated with wonderful scatological enthusiasm, 'May I always have it off as well as I had it off here!' Subsequent generations have produced their own heroes, notably the ubiquitous Kilroy who has apparently been here, there and everywhere since the middle of the twentieth century. The origin of the famous line, 'Kilroy was Here,' is undoubtedly American and can be reliably traced to the hand of a shipyard inspector, James J Kilroy, whose job was to inspect ships being built in Quincy, Massachusetts, during the Second World War. Before long, the phrase had spread far beyond the bounds of the shipyard and was often accompanied by a simple sketch of a face with a large nose peering over a wall.

Today, the folklore surrounding graffiti is multiplying by the year, and in New York recently a number of doors, which had been covered in words and pictures by several legendary artists, including Keith Haring, Jean-Michel Basquiat and Fab Five Freddie were sold at auction, with one particular apartment door fetching more than £15,000. Some lines of graffiti have even inspired the titles of bestselling books and theatrical productions, including Edward Albee's *Who's Afraid of Virginia Woolf?* – found in a subway – while Anthony Newley spotted the title of his play, *Stop The World, I Want To Get Off* on a London wall. The examples that I have collected here are probably not going to generate quite such fame and fortune, but their literary humour is certainly priceless!

Agatha Christie has died — whodunnit?

Alas, poor Yorlik, I knew him backwards

A dictionary is the only place where success comes before work

All men eat but Fu Manchu

Alma Nack is with Old Moore

Anagrams lure, OK

Anyone for Tennyson?

Auden was very Audenry

Back in a minute — Godot

Bad spellers of the world, untie!

Bede thrills

Barad-dur boot boys rule Middle
Earth, OK?

Barnardo homes hate Sherlock Holmes

Biggles flies open

Come back Godot, all is forgiven

Confucius he say too much

Concentrate on Rousseau instead of your Trousseau — Sorry, I Kant

Cunnilingus spoken here

The days of good English has went

Dr Strangelove; or, How I Learned to
Love the Bum

Dracula — your Bloody Mary is ready

Edith Sitwell is a transvestite!

Fiction is a fact

Flash Gordon exposes himself to all
sorts of perils for mankind

Forever amber — the story of a broken traffic light

Frodo has been busted

Fucque Braque

Genitals Prefer Blondes

George Orwell was an optimist

Graffiti is squatters' writes

God is dead — Nietzsche.
Nietzsche is dead — God

Have you heard of the Guinness Record of Books?

Henry James must have fucked someone!

Henry Miller is a virgin

Herman Melville eats blubber

Home Rule for Wales — and Moby Dick for King!

Humpty Dumpty was pushed

I am, therefore I think — Is this putting Descartes before the horse?

I choked Linda Lovelace

I thought Fellatio was a character in Hamlet until I discovered Smirnoff

If God had Tipp-Ex [white-out] he could blot out the mistakes

If pornography relieves sexual frustration — give cookbooks to the hungry

Illiterates watch this space

Immanuel Kant but Genghis Khan

In France do they play scrabble with french letters?

Isaac Newton counts on his fingers

Is Hamlet the son of Piglet?

I love Margaret Holmes — Good Lord, Watson, so do I!

I thought nausea was a novel by sartre until I discovered scrumpy

'It's a lie – I was never here,' Kilroy

I've been hanging around here for ages — Godot

I wandered lonely as a cloud because I had B.O.

James Bond Rules OOK?

Jesus Christ is alive and well – signing copies of the
Bible at Foyles

Killjoy was here — but his pencil broke

Kilroy was a Laplander

Marghanita Laski was a Bunny Girl

MI5 – the origin of spieses

Mr Kipling writes exceedingly good books

Lassie Kills Chickens

Latin is the language of the dead

Literature sets the world aflame – fire the Soho
porn shops

Little Red Riding Hood is a Russian contraceptive

The Marquis de Sade really knew how to hurt a guy

Marshall McLuhan is print-orientated

Mary Poppins shouldn't fly around without knickers

Mickey Mouse is gay — true, Donald Duckie

Moby Dick is a honky

1978 makes 1984 look like 1967

Norman Mailer is the master of the single entendre

Oedipus was the first man to plug the generation gap

Oedipus — phone your mother

Ogden Nash is trash

The only good books are read ones

Othello was a bigot

Oust Proust

P-P-Patrick Campbell ru-ru-ru-rules

The penis mightier than the sword

Perry Mason bribes judges

Peter Pan is alive and well in Greenwich Village
— with Tinkerbell

Pick up a penguin — and hit its head against a wall

Poetry is when every line starts with a capital letter

Printers do it and don't wrinkle
the sheets

Pussy Galore for president

Quasimodo — that name rings a bell

Quentin Crisp is straight

Roget's Thesaurus rules —
dominates, regulates, all right,
OK

Roo loves Pooh

Samuel Beckett is Krapp

Save energy — write slowly

school for Vandals

Sexton Blake loves to tinker

Shakespeare brought home the bacon

Shakespeare sucked Bacon dry

shakespeare used bard language —
but Anne hath a way with him

Sherlock Holmes for deduction — Casanova for
reproduction

Socrates eats hemlock

Superman gets into Clark Kent's pants every morning

This Wall was dictated by Mr
Chad and signed in his absence

Timothy Leary is an alcholic

Tolkien is hobbit-forming — So is Dildo Baggins!

Top Copy — no boobs please. Bottom Copy — bum's
the word

Typographers rule, OQ

The waste basket is mightier than the pen

A watched proverb butters no parsnips!

Watership Down — You've read the book, seen the film,
now eat the pie

What makes sammy run?
Laxative

Who will rid me of this turbulent Proust?

Who was the poet lying in the sun? Robert Browning

A wire tap turns James Bond on

The wisest two words in the
dictionary are shut and up

Words mean nothing today

You Tarzan. Migraine

You're a better man than I, Mrs Dinn — Gunga

Yorick is a numb skull

One would think to read all this wit,
That shakespeare himself came here to shit.

The Cleaner's work has been in vain —
The Phantom Writer's struck again!

And, finally:

This wall will shortly be available in paperback.

Edgar Allan Poe was a Curdling Writer

A Syllabus of Literary Howlers

For several years while I was working in publishing I lived near Highgate and there first heard about a legendary collector and writer on howlers, Cecil Hunt. He had earned the soubriquet 'The Howler King of Highgate' as a result of a series of books he had compiled beginning in 1927 with *Howlers* and swelling to half a dozen volumes by the time he reached *Hand-Picked Howlers* in 1937 and *Ripe Howlers* two years later. Hunt's friend Edmund Blampied amusingly illustrated all of these books. What also interested me about 'the King' was that he had started collecting his material while living in Enfield, my home town. It seemed almost inevitable that our paths should cross, although by the sixties all of his titles were long out of print and it took me several years to obtain second-hand copies.

Cecil Hunt's early sources were mainly junior schools, but he went on to include grammar schools and even, on occasions, universities. I had hours of fun dipping into these books, and one particular item set me off collecting those with a literary inspiration. It was written by a London schoolboy, apparently: 'Writers are very strange because teacher says tails come out of their heads.' To Cecil Hunt, these errors from the classroom and the examination hall represented a 'form of humour that is without malice and is alive with humanity'. He did not feel it necessary to add that all the perpetrators were, of course, hilariously *wrong!*

What 'The Howler King of Highgate' initiated, I have continued in more recent years, collecting literary howlers from all over the world and adding material from such diverse sources as evening classes and correspondence courses – revealing that adults can slip up just as comically as youngsters. Even examiners can occasionally get it wrong, as one paper sent to me demonstrated: 'Examinations may be written or vice versa.' My selection begins with Shakespeare, primarily because the poor fellow has probably suffered more from literary howlers than anyone else . . .

The greatest writer of the Renaissance was William Shakespeare. He was born in the year 1564, supposedly on his birthday. He wrote tragedies, comedies and hysterectomies, all in Islamic pentameter.

Five of Shakespeare's best plays are *Macbeth*, *The Mikado*, *Quo Vadis*, *San Toy* and *The Sign of the Cross*.

Shakespeare married Anne Hathaway who, it seems, lived up to her name and had her own way and gave Shakespeare a hot time of it.

Shakespeare lived in Windsor with his merry wives.

There are some passages in Shakespeare's works that are quite pretty, such as 'Spoil the rod and spare the child' and lots of others.

The Bard of Avon was Oliver Cromwell.

In Shakespeare's *A Midsummer Night's Dream*, Puck turns Bottom's head into an ass.

In the play, Bottom, as his name suggests, behaves in a very bumptious manner.

Romeo met Juliet for the first time at the massacred ball.

Romeo had to keep walking under Juliet's bed. This is one of his greatest tragedies.

Romeo's last wish was to be laid by Juliet.

The Merchant of Venice was a famous Italian who bought and sold canal boats.

Shakespeare often said, 'Go to!' but having been on the stage he knew where to stop.

'To be or not to be; that is the question.' Nobody knows what this means because many words Shakespeare wrote now mean something else.

No one has yet succeeded in edifying the Dark Lady of the Sonnets.

Q: I what circumstances does the Fourth Act of
Hamlet begin?
A: It commences immediately after the Third
Act.

The heroine of The Merchant of Venice
is a lady called Portico.

Macbeth was Dick Turpin's horse.

Prospero had a faithful friend called Gorgonzola.

Hamlet stabbed Ophelia's father
Polyphemus who was hiding behind the
fireplace.

Macduff said he had never been born of a woman because he had been
stolen when he was a baby.

Bacon was the man who thought he wrote
Shakespeare.

Bowdler was the writer who made
Shakespeare understandable to the
masses.

Anonymous is the man who writes all
the poems which are not signed.

Cyclops wrote the Encyclopaedia.

There were three great Greek historians,
Ulysses, Circe and Bacchus.

Ovid wrote a poem called Medea which was lost unfortunately.

Plato's Republic *was another name for the infernal regions.*

Mephistopheles was a Greek comic poet.

Homer wrote *The Oddity.*

Virgil was in love with a girl named Enid and wrote lots of books about her.

Livid was a famous Roman poet.

Socrates died from an overdose of wedlock.

Algebra is the wife of Euclid.

The *Compleat Angler* is another name for Euclid, who wrote all about angles.

Esau was a man who wrote fables and sold his copyright for a mess of pottage.

The Kodak is the Bible of the Mohammedans.

In the first book of the Bible, *Guinessis, Adam and Eve were created from an apple tree.*

Moses went up on Mount Cyanide to get the Ten Commandments.

According to the Bible, Jesus was born because Mary had an immaculate contraption.

Gutenberg invented removable type and the Bible.

John Wycliff's great work was the translation of the Bible into Middle English because he thought the people would be more likely to understand the English as spoken in the Midlands.

William the Conqueror is one of our foremost authors and wrote the Domesday Book.

The Domesday Book is a book which tells about the animals in the country. It has got in it how many tadpoles there are in a pond.

Cicero was banished to Macedonia where he wrote the Book of Lamentations.

Palsy is a kind of new writer's dance.

A fairy tale is something that never happened a long time ago.

A sentence is a short conversation.

A quotation is the answer to a division sum.

The definition of 'prose' is men who get paid for playing cricket.

In every book there is a hero and a heroine and they are called the heroic couplet.

The hero of the story was clad in a shining suet of arm.

Autobiography is the history of motor cars.

The objective of 'He' is 'She'.

The feminine of friar is none.

Q: Give three adverbs ending in '-where'.
A: Somewhere, Nowhere and Earthenwhere.

'ster' is a feminine suffix, as will be seen in spinster, monster and sterile.

A strong verb is one that changes its vowels eternally.

A passive verb is when the subject is the sufferer, as 'I am loved'.

A sonnet is a group of words out of which fourteen lines are made.

A metaphor is a kind of signalling used chiefly for long distances.

Poetic License was a License that used to be granted to poets allowing them to recite their poems in public houses.

Rambo was a famous French poet

A catalogue is a dialogue by four people.

The death of Julius Caesar was foretold by a shower of metaphors.

Alfred the Great started a Chronicle and this existed until recently as a morning newspaper.

In the reign of King George the Second according to the history books the good old days were taking place.

Pepys wrote a diary and invented a cough drop.

Edmond Dantes was an Italian poet who wrote tales about Hades and eternal fire.

James the First wrote a few books which were unfit to read.

In 1663, Milton married and afterwards he wrote *Paradise Lost*. Later his wife died and he then wrote *Paradise Regained*.

Gray's Elegy was written in a churchyard in many talkings and should be kept for ever, from first verse to last.

Chaucer was the father of English pottery.

Chaucer wrote the Arabian Knights who were holy men like Prince Arthur and made pilgrimages to Canterbury and told tales round a table.

When Chaucer described the Prioress as amiable of port he meant she was fond of wine.

Milton's poems are pleasant to read, but being strict Puritan throughout the whole of the poems, there is nothing to promote laughter.

Luther burnt the Papal Bull and then the fat was in the fire.

The Venerable Bede wrote an Elastical History.

Oliver Goldsmith was one of the greatest poets and wrote 'The Unauthorised Virgin' and many others.

The 'Deserted Traveller' is the most important of Goldsmith's works.

Lady Jane Grey did not want to be queen, she would much rather read all day.

Coleridge was a retired mariner who took to verse and wrote *Ku-Klux-Klan*.

Kubla Khan is an American secret society.

Sir Walter Scott was imprisoned in the Tower because he could not pay his debts. While he was there he wrote the Waverley Novels, but he was afterwards burnt alive.

Charles Darwin was the originator of the human species and wrote a lot about it.

Darwin was the author of a famous book called *Tarzan of the Apes*.

Ganymede and Runnymede were two characters by Charles Dickens.

In *Great Expectations*, Miss Haversham puts herself into conclusion.

The only Englishman who became Pope of Rome was Nicholas Nickleby.

Bill Sikes and his friends all went to Widdicome Fair on the back of a horse and on the way back it died.

In the olden days, little boys didn't have any fathers and mothers, so Oliver Twist had to be born in a workhouse.

The ghost of Bob Marley visited Ebenezer Scrooge.

When Marley's Ghost appeared bound in chains, Scrooge said, 'Are you a punk?'

Edgar Allan Poe was a curdling writer.

Edgar Allan Poe was born in Boston in 1809 and was found unconscious. Three days later, he died in 1849.

Twenty-thousand Leagues Under the Sea is a book about a lot of underwater football teams.

In *Little Women* Amy had an air of refinery about her.

Harriet Beecher Stowe's famous novel about the evils of slavery was called *Uncle Tom's Cabinet.*

If it had not been for Rabbie Burns's intemperance we might have had him with us yet.

Madame Bovary's problem was that she couldn't make love in the concrete.

Robinson Crusoe was a sailor who got stuck on an uninhibited island without even a television.

As he grew older, Wordsworth went out one evening because he felt the call of nature.

The poetry of Wordsworth is too full of thoughts to be natural. His descriptions of sunsets are natural but rural.

Oliver Wendell Holmes was a very profligate writer.

F Scott Fitzgerald's *The Great Gatsby*
exemplified American culture in the 1920s to
a tea.

H G Wells' Outline of History *is a
veritable millstone on the road to learning.*

In 1957, Eugene O'Neill won a
Pullet Surprise.

The Sherlock Holmes stories were written by Arthur Cohen Doyle.

At the start of *The Grapes of Wrath,* Oklahoma
has been hit by a dust bowl.

**Jake Barnes in *The Sun Also Rises,*
was injured in the groin region
and was impudent for the rest of
his life.**

The theme of *The Catcher in the Rye* is that
Holden Caulfield leaves the world of childhood
and enters the world of adultery.

A Plagiarist is a writer of plays.

Letters in sloping type are in hysterics.

Spoonerisms were proposals of marriage made by a man after that name.

An antidote is a funny story you have heard before.

Euphemism is a thing which is not done by people, e.g. mew, woof or cock-a-doodle.

An epic poem is a poem in which the words are of one syllable.

A collective noun is a noun that covers everything, such as clothing, umbrella, bandstand, etc.

A mixed metaphor means putting the wrong halves of proverbs together, such as 'Too many cooks make an ill wind' or 'A spoilt broth blows nobody any good'.

One of the best proverbs to remember is that kind hearts are better than cornets.

Terminology is a science which deals with the ends of words.

The author's story is very aboriginal.

When it used to say in books that a man carried his mistress's favour on his arm, it meant that he carried the baby on his arm.

In crime stories, the detective is a man who searches out the mysteries of things in his private clothes.

Cynics are men who believe in fairy stories.

A comma is what a medium falls into.

A colon is a punctuation mark in
the human body.

Ambiguity means writing the truth when you
don't want to.

Poets no longer wear long hair and dirty clothes, but they still expect
people to read what they have written.

A poet's swan song is his last gasp.

The Bodleian is a type of harp.

The Highway Code is a book of rules for
walkers who are run over.

A lot of printing paper is now made from Esperanto grass.

An appendix is the portion of a
book that nobody has yet discovered
to be of any use.

Eight

The Jockstrap Position

Pardon, My Mondegreen Is Showing

My first experience of the mondegreen was when my daughter was born. Still exhilarated by the events in the hospital where my wife had given birth to our third child, I rang our various relatives and then called the office of my current publisher. Speaking to his receptionist – a woman I knew from numerous visits to the office – I burbled, 'I've got a baby daughter.' The news was greeted by total silence. Puzzled, but not upset, as not everyone loves babies, I asked to speak to my publisher-friend. After he had congratulated me enthusiastically and asked after mother and child, I told him I had been a little bit surprised by the lack of response by his receptionist. Within moments of putting down the phone, it rang again with the self-same woman on the other end of the line. She was terribly embarrassed, she said, because she often had to deal with egocentric authors. 'I thought you said "*I am a famous author!*"' she confessed.

What that receptionist had suffered was a 'homophonic misunderstanding', or misheard name, phrase or saying. In other words, a mondegreen. There has been some debate among linguists as to how this expression was born. I am inclined to accept that the writer Sylvia Wright first used it in an article for the *Atlantic Monthly* in 1954. In this she explained how she had misheard a folk song, 'The Bonny Earl of Moray' when she was a child. The words actually sung were, 'They had slain the Earl of Moray and laid him on the green.' What she *though* she heard was, 'They had slain the Earl of Moray and Lady Mondegreen.' Here is a selection of just such misunderstandings named after the eponymous lady, which I have collected over the years as well as others from friends or newspapers and magazines and in the book trade.

Hark, how the author had a favourite daughter – a misunderstanding of that famous hymn, 'Hark the Herald Angels Sing'.

Glady, my cross-eyed bear – from the famous Sunday School hymn 'Gladly, My Cross I Bear'.

While shepherds washed their socks by night – one of a number of Christmas carol variations.

Round John Virgin and mother and child – another Christmas carol favourite.

Deck the halls with Buddy Holly – A pop star becomes mixed with 'Deck the Halls with Boughs of Holly'.

We three Kings of porridge and tar – variation of 'We Three Kings'.

Radiate meat from your holy place – mondegreen from 'Silent Night'.

May your days be merry in brine – Bing Crosby's classic, 'White Christmas'.

What fun it is to write and sing a slaying song to knives – 'What fun it is to ride and sing a sleighing song tonight' from another classic, 'Jingle Bells'.

Six geezers laying – the halfway point of 'The Twelve Days of Christmas'.

Feed the worms – from the Band Aid hit, 'Do They Know It's Christmas?'

Starkle, starkle little twink, who the hell am I do you think? – the inebriate's version of 'Twinkle, Twinkle, Little Star'.

I am not so think as you drunk I am – also from the tipsy repertoire of mondegreens.

A nude dame to see – variation of 'A newborn king to see' from 'The Little Drummer Boy'.

Miniza seen the glory of the coming of the Lord – opening line from 'Mine Eyes Have Seen the Coming Of The Lord'.

BLONDES PREFER
GENTLEMEN

A SATIRE

BY

 " MELITA NOOSE."

The Shaming of the True – even Shakespeare is not safe from misunderstanding.

Hell hath no fury like a woman's corns – from William Congreve's *The Mourning Bride*, 'Hell hath no fury like a woman scorned.'

Double, double, toilet trouble – the witches' chorus from *Macbeth*.

She Stoops to Conga – a child's library request for Oliver Goldsmith's *She Stoops to Conquer*.

Rap City in Blue – mondegreen for the George Gershwin classic, 'Rhapsody in Blue'.

Box of puppies – newspaper column reporting on 'Boxer Puppies'.

Touchdown – the regularly abused name of the clown in *As You Like It* by William Shakespeare.

Donkey Hote – Miguel Cervantes' famous novel, *Don Quixote*.

Up the struggle naughty bailiff! – from the poet Arthur Clough's line, 'Say not the struggle nought availeth'.

The Organ of the Species – Charles Darwin's pioneering work, *The Origin of the Species*.

Ancient Squirrels in the Dead Sea – famous *Times* story about the discovery of the Dead Sea Scrolls.

The Screwing of the Tern – misreporting of Henry James's ghost story, *The Turn of the Screw.*

French the Lieutenant's Woman – the John Fowles classic, *The French Lieutenant's Woman.*

Lame is Rob – the Victor Hugo classic which has become a smash hit as a musical, *Les Miserables.*

A Sale of Two Titties – indelicate rendering of Dickens's *A Tale of Two Cities.*

Reverend A T B McGowan from Mallaig and the Small Aisles – another famous *Times* mondegreen.

American Seat – a popular folk dance actually entitled, *A Merry Conceit.*

The girl with colitis goes by – from The Beatles song, 'Lucy in the Sky with Diamonds'.

The ants are my friends – variation of Bob Dylan's line, 'The answer, my friends, is blowin' in the wind.'

've thrown custard in her face – the great line from *My Fair Lady*, 'I've grown accustomed to her face.'

Solicitor and not a republic – a journalists' favourite for 'Solicitor and Notary Public'.

Quantities of Air – another professional variation for Quantity Surveyor.

Farm assistant – the occupation given for a pharmacist joining the army.

He's cutting off his nose despite his face – another famous saying gets the treatment.

Brazilians in adversity – symptoms shown by patients as described in a Sunday newspaper medical column.

Crazy military organisation – the Church Lad's Brigade referred to in a story as a 'quasi' band of youths.

The Lyin' Bitch in the Wardrobe – the classic C S Lewis fantasy novel, *The Lion, the Witch and the Wardrobe*.

Captain de Milly's Violin – request in a bookshop for Louis De Bernières' bestseller, *Captain Corelli's Mandolin*.

The Pen Club in Wigan? – the response to an enquiry for the famous journalist's hostelry, the Wig and Pen Club in London.

Heathfield Wreck Tree – a postal error for Heathfield Rectory in Somerset.

The Countess of Ayr is coming to tea – Scottish mistake for the visit of a County Surveyor.

Are you strong enough? – answer to a request for a plate of Pork Stroganoff.

Requires help for three awful hours a week – newspaper insertion for assistance 'three or four hours a week'.

Sexy Quality of Women – inspired by a newspaper discussion on Sex Equality.

Stay Colder Pensions – enquiry after the government document on Stake Holder Pensions.

Haddock-stirring committee – a government official's invitation to an 'ad hoc' steering committee.

The Greek Ambassador sauntered into view – a Foreign Office memo that should have read 'The Greek Ambassador sought an interview.'

Jockstrap Position – phrase from a leading physician's paper for a medical journal misusing the word juxtaposition.

Wild Sunshine – newsprint muddle of Terence Rattigan's play, *While the Sun Shines*.

Call I love you, White Radio – a message to Isle of Wight MP, Andrew Turner, to ring his local broadcasting station.

Roger's Choir – newspaper billing for comedy magician Roger Squires.

Dear J Nasher – form of greeting on a letter sent to the actress Jane Asher.

Miss Hazel Hurst – another error in correspondence to writer Dick Hazelhurst.

Welcome to the Squeen's Peach – statement by Prime Minister Tony Blair in the Houses of Parliament in June 2001.

But deliver us some email – recent addition to the mondegreen canon as the last line of the Lord's Prayer.

Nine

Thou Shalt Commit Adultery

The Bible and the Printer's Devil

I read somewhere that there is only one joke in the Bible. I am not sure *what* story is being referred to, but in actual fact the book contains quite a number of amusing episodes – ranging from those about the Old Testament prophets who indulged in eating scrolls (Ezekiel, iii) and hiding underwear beneath rocks (Jeremiah, xiii) to the comic misadventures of Balaam's ass (Numbers, xxii). Jesus also had a ready store of one-liners for suitable moments, including such gems as, 'The poor always ye have with you' and 'the blind leading the blind'. I'm also unable to resist smiling at another particular line from Job xxxi, 35: 'Oh that mine adversary had written a book.'

The Bible itself has also inspired some amusing stories among the literary fraternity, like that concerning Thomas Mitchell who was discovered on his deathbed reading a copy and when asked what he was doing, replied: 'Looking for a loophole.' There was also the dying classical scholar, Arthur Bernard

Cook, who while he was being read to from the 121st Psalm protested, 'That is a mistranslation!' And there is something irredeemably comic about the eccentric Victorian vicar of Bremhill, William Bowles, who presented one of his friends with a copy of the Bible inscribed, 'With the Author's Compliments'. And I must not forget to mention the enterprising publisher who not so long ago advertised his edition of the Bible with a jingle that ran:

> Holy Scripture, Writ Divine,
> Leather-bound at one and nine.
> Satan trembles when he sees,
> Bibles sold as cheap as these.

Over the centuries, the Bible has been published in countless editions and translations, not overlooking those in shorthand – issued by Jeremy Rich, c. 1665 – and even hieroglyphics in 1785, when small pictures were used instead of specific words and phrases. The Bible has also suffered more than most books at the hands of its printers and there is, for example, a copy of an eighteenth-century edition on display in Westminster Abbey which is aptly known as the 'Printer's Bible'. A line in Psalms, cxix, 161, reads, 'Printers have persecuted me without a cause.' The word should, of course, be 'Princes'. This is, though, by no means the worst misprint, and here are some of the most amusing examples of the intervention of the Printer's Devil that have resulted in some *very* Unauthorised Versions of the good book.

And Adam and Eve sewed fig leaves together and made themselves breeches [clothes].
                                        Genesis, iii, 7 – Geneva, 1534

Thou shalt not need to be afraid for any bugges [terror] by night.
                                        Psalms, xci, 5 – Coverdale, 1535

Blessed are the placemakers [peacemakers].
Matthew, v, 9 – London, 1562

Christ condemneth [commendeth] the poore widdowe.
Luke, xxi, 1 – London, 1562

Is there no treacle [balm] in Gilead.
Jeremiah, viii, 22 – Coverdale, 1568

Then said Judas [Jesus] unto the twelve.
John, vi, 67 – London, 1611

Thou shalt [not] commit adultery.
Exodus, xx, 14 – Blackfriars, 1632

The fool hath said in his heart, there is [no] God.
Psalms, xiv, 1 – London, 1634

Her sins, which are many, are forgotten [forgiven].
Luke, vii, 47 – Cambridge, 1638

Know ye that the unrighteous shall [not] inherit the kingdom of God?
I Corinthians, vi, 9 – London, 1653

Neither yield ye your members as instruments of [un]righteousness unto sin.
Romans, vi, 13 – London, 1653

I have seen thine adversaries [adulteries].
Jeremiah, xiii, 27 – London, 1682

Therefore deliver up their children to the swine [famine].
Jeremiah, vxiii, 21 – London, 1682

E S S A Y

UPON
IMPROVING and ADDING
TO THE
STRENGTH
OF
GREAT-BRITAIN and *IRELAND*
BY
FORNICATION

JUSTIFYING
The same from SCRIPTURE and REASON.

By a Young CLERGYMAN.

Omne tulit punctum qui miscuit utile dulci.   Hor.

Gen. Chap. i. v. 28. *And God blessed them, and said unto them, Be fruitful, and multiply, and replenish the Earth.* Chap. ix. v. 1. *And God Blessed Noah and his Sons, and said unto them, Be fruitful, and multiply, and replenish the Earth.* v. 7. *And you, be ye fruitful, and multiply, bring forth abundantly in the Earth, and multiply therein.*

LONDON:
Printed in the Year M.DCC.XXXV.

And if the latter husband [h]ate her.
Deuteronomy, xxiv, 3 – London, 1682

For without are dogs, and scorers [sorcerers].
Revelation, xxii, 15 – Clarendon, 1702

Behold, thou art made whole: sin on [no] more.
John, v, 14 – Oxford, 1716

The Parable of the Vinegar [Vineyard].
Luke, xx – London, 1724

The sting [string] of his tongue.
Mark, vii, 35 – Edinburgh, 1747

Ye Blind guides which strain out [at] a gnat.
Matthew, xxii, 24 – Cambridge, 1760

Their land brought forth frogs, yea seven [even] in their King's chamber.
Psalms, v, 30 – London, 1778

Let the children first be killed [filled].
Mark, vii, 27 – Winchester, 1795

These are murderers [murmurers].
Jude, xvi, 16 – Canterbury, 1801

For the flesh lusteth after [against] the Spirit.
Galatians, v, 17 – London, 1804

But thy son that shall come forth out of thy lions [loins].
I Kings, viii, 19 – London, 1804

The murderers shall surely be put together [to death].
Numbers, xxxv, 18 – London, 1804

I discharge [charge] thee before God

Timothy, v, 21 – London, 180◌

Who hath ears to [h]ear, let him hear.

Matthew, xiii, 43 – Cambridge, 180◌

Woe to the idol [idle] shepherd.

Zechariah, xi, 17 – London, 180◌

If any man come to me, and hate not his father and mother, yea an◌ his own wife [life] also

Luke, xiv, 26 – London, 181◌

And it shall come to pass, that the fishes [fishers] shall stand.

Ezekiel, xiv, 19 – London, 181◌

Shall I bring to the birth, and not cease [cause] to bring forth.

Isiah, xvi, 9 – Oxford, 182◌

And Rebekah arose, and her camels [damsels]

Genesis, xxiv, 61 – London, 182◌

Intending after Esther [Easter].

Acts, xii, 4 – London, 182◌

For Christ also hath once offered [suffered] for our sins

Peter, iii, 18 – London, 182◌

Rejoice and be exceeding dad [glad]

Matthew, v, 12 – York, 186◌

A man may not marry his grandmother's wife.

Table of Affinity, Oxford University Press, 192◌

Pay [Pray] for peace.

Psalm 122, 6 – Jerusalem Bible, 1966

To conclude this chapter on the Bible, here are three examples of how it has recently been modernised for new generations of readers:

Jesus wis born at Bethlehem in Judea i the days o king Herod, and it wis nae time efter his birth or a curn spaemen frae the Aist cam tae Jerusalem an begoud speirin, 'Whaur is the King of Jews at hes come hame eenou?'

The New Testament in Scots, 2001

The Angel of the Lord said to the shepherds in the field, 'Stop looking like a bunch of stunned mullets.'

The Aussie Bible, 2002

i'll tell you who'll laugh last, said jesus, the people who know they're a mess.

The Street Bible, 2003

Ten

English as She Is Wrotten

A Misguided Tour of Translation

One of the first books I was commissioned to write back in the sixties was a guide to the Channel Islands and my wife-to-be and I spent an idyllic few weeks touring the main islands situated just off the coast of France collecting information. The book duly appeared and was successful enough to be reprinted a couple of times. However, the problem was always keeping up-to-date with information and I must admit that there were one or two facts and even a couple of translations from the French that were incorrect and haunt me to this day. The publisher, though, did not receive a single letter of complaint.

The guidebook industry has become big business in the last couple of centuries as methods of transport have improved and the desire of people to travel further afield has increased every year. Alongside the growth of this interest have come an ever-creasing number of guidebooks to inform and instruct tourists about the places to visit. One of the greatest pitfalls for such guides lies in translation, which has resulted in some glaring errors, not to mention very amusing mistakes. This fact was familiar to Charles Berlitz, the man who founded the famous institution bearing his name, Berlitz Language Schools, and has recently been commented on again by his grandson, also Charles Berlitz, in his book, *Native Tongues*, in which he offers many little-known facts and anecdotes about languages. Among the most fascinating is that *German* could have been the official language of the United States if the proposal had not been defeated by just one vote at the Continental Conference in Philadelphia. He also lists a number of curious examples of the foibles of translation, citing the well-known English proverb 'Don't count your chickens before they are hatched' becoming in German, 'You can't hang people before you've caught them,' and the delicate matter of complimenting a Japanese woman on her beauty where her face must be compared to 'an egg with eyes'.

Such variations in the nuances of words and phrases have led to some comic mistranslations, as you will discover in this chapter.

The Elements of French Translation

John Perrin (1820)

This book, published in Paris early in the nineteenth century, is one of the earliest I have been able to trace and was evidently popular, as the publisher claims it ran to 21 editions. The following phrases were apparently repeated through many of the printings and Mr Perrins's work might fairly be said to have set the standard for all the writers and publishers who followed in his footsteps.

Ayez soin de la retaper proprement – Take care to cock it up neatly.
Cortège – A small house in the country.
Déshabiller – To give up a bad habit.
Du jambon cru – What was supposed to be ham.

Elle a mal au coeur – She is rotten to the core.

Elles sont venues – The girls have come.

Emporté par la colère – Carried off by the collar.

L'Esposé du matin – The Morning Bride.

Feu la reine – Shoot the Queen.

Hors d'oeuvre – Out of work.

Huile d'olivier – Oily oblivion.

Il a un crêpe au chapeau – He has crept into his hat.

Il se précipite vers le cabinet – He hurries to the booking-office.

J'ai hâte de l'embrasser – I hate to embrace her.

La lueur argentée de la lune – The moneyed light of the moon.

La jeune fille avait acquis plus de poids dans les conseils de la famille – According to the girl's family, she was bought more by weight.

Laisser-faire – An idle French woman.

Le livre est un bon un – The book is a good one.

Menage à trois – To share the burden.

Mes souvenirs sont peu précis – My recollections are precious few.

Prenez garde que votre cheval ne prenne pas le mors entre les dents – Take care that your horse does not die of the toothache.

Savoir faire – To know a good thing.

Spectacles théâtrales – Opera glasses.

Un homme mange plus d'une femme – A man eats more than a woman.

Vous pouvez compter qu'il sera retapé dans le dernier goût – You may depend that it will be cocked up in the neatest taste.

New Guide of the Conversation in Portuguese and English
Professor Pedro Carolino (1869)

The Professor's extraordinary volume has become notorious for its sub-title, *English As She Is Wrotten*, although the author was undoubtedly proud of his little book 'for the care what we wrote him, and for her typographical correction'. Nothing is known about Carolino beyond the evident fact that his grasp of English was rudimentary at best and the omens for the book were hardly good when it was first published in Paris using a printer in Peking who only compounded the mistakes. I have selected what I believe is one of the funniest sections, dealing with writing and books.

The Writing

Sit down by desk, you shall find every thing there what it must for to write.

This paper blot.

There is another. Without doubt its are agreables news to which you propose you self to answer?

Its are some commerce letters at which I have to answer. Yours pens have any notches, and its spit.

How do you like its? Will you its are fine or broad.

I forget its too fine. Don't you have a penknife? I go to make a pen my self.

Here is one, but I think shall it want setting.

I won't me also a wafer or some sealing wax and a seal.

In this drawer, there is all that, falding stick, rule, scraper, sand, etc.

I am going to fold it, put it the envelope and write the address.

There it is ready. When do part the post?

There is the postman. I go to put it.

The Books and of the Reading

What read you there?

A romance wrote very well, translated of the English, entitled The Independent.

Do you like the reading good deal too many which seem me?

This is to me a amusement.

You have there a library too many considerable, it is a proof your love for the learnings.

I have good many books I do not read, and I do not than to consult.

Are you in the reach of the good literature?

I think to have read every thing what have some reputation.

I see that yours books are almost all binded in morocco leather, gilt edge.

I have also any bindings in calf and on sheep leather.

With a Bookseller

What is there in new's literature?

Little or almost nothing, if not appears any thing of note.

And yet one imprint many deal.

That is true, but what it is imprinted. Some news papers, pamphlets, and others ephemural pieces, here is.

But why, you and another bookseller, you does not to imprint some good works?

There is a reason for that, it is that you cannot sell its.

The actual liking of the public is depraved, they do not read who for to amuse one's self and but to instruct one's.

But the letter's men who cultivate the arts and the sciences they can't to pass without the books.

A little learneds are happies enough for to may to satisfy their fancies on the literature.

What is the price of this fine Shakespeare edition? A hundred and fifty franks.

Have you found the Buffoon who I had call for?

Idiotisms and Proverbs

Here are some blue stories.

To put the points on the i.

The walls have hearsay.

To buy a cat in pocket.

He is like the fish into the water.

To eat of the cow mad.

The necessity don't know the law.

To meet any-one nose at nose.

Four eyes does see better than two.

What come in for me for an ear yet out for another.

After the paunch comes the dance.

He has the throat paved.

To pay one's self for her hands.

Every one for him, and God for all.

The diffidence is mother of security.

The hands are to itch to him.

That which feel one's snotty, blow one's nose.

He sin in trouble water.

Belly famished has no ears.

He is beggar as a church rat.

He is not so devil as he is black.

It is better be single as a bad company.

He has turned the heels.

To go of bad in worse.

It before that you marry look twice.

In the country of blinds, the one eyed men are kings.

Of the hand to mouth, one loose often the soup.

A thing is tell, and another thing is make.

The dress don't make the monk.

Drunk as a hole.

All what shine is not gold.

He is not understand the jest.

English as She Is Taught

Mark Twain (1887)

There is no evidence that Mark Twain read Professor Carolino's book, but he was clearly aware of the increasing library of error-strewn guidebooks. As a former printer and editor of a newspaper, the *Virginia City Enterprise*, he knew all about the vagaries of language and the idiosyncrasies of the press. Here are a few choice items from his section, 'Some Quaint Definitions of Words'.

> Aborigines – a system of mountains.
> Amenable – any thing that is mean.
> Equestrian – one who asks questions.
> Franchise – anything belonging to the French.
> Parasite – a kind of umbrella.
> Plagiarist – a writer of plays.

How to Do and Say in England

Punch (1936)

The sub-title of this 'guide' once again gave away its intentions: *A Trim Kompaktikum for Students of English Talk and Society Behaviourism. (Made in Germany.)* It came complete with an 'Appreciative' by the Nazi propaganda minister, Dr Goebbels: 'No German should circulate with not the Best People in any country. The informations in this book are a revelation of the first water, the commodious idioms provided are strikktli Aryan and the Englisch is unik.' It later transpired that the work was a spoof by a *Punch* contributor, Anthony Robertson, and certainly one of its funniest sections dealt with 'Englisch Humoristics' including 'Slapp-stick, Slapp-bach, Ironics, Witty Talkin' and, especially, 'Pun-fun'.

A modicum of the Best People assert that they eschew punning and deem it a social solecismus. They vilify the author of such and cry, 'O-pun the door' in a manner to indicate resentment and groan outwardly. So take care of yourself before putting forward a dictum couched in this style.

You may find, though, that along of the Very Best People that money can buy, it is more of a dasched good proposition altogether indeed, but even here depreciation is sometimes of necessity and it is wise to be slightly shamefaced.

'Really, I talk away in puns and twos, sixteen to the dozen,' might be a good thing to aver after releasing a remarque somewhat too far-flung, in an attempt to be excusable. Or: 'Pardon my remarques, they slip out all too glibly for me!'

Puns, of course, are chokes in which the two main words are resembular. Owing to the menacing attitude towards them, it is valuable to learn a set of phrases. Thus it would never do to shout 'Ho! Ho!

What a delicious pun, I think!' only to hear the Best People complaining.

These dictums are fairly safe to use:

'He has punned! Ghastly! Does he indeed take us for not-wits?' (To be said in a confidential sideways to someone else.)

'Did you make that pun with aforethought or was it just a terrible accident?' (Await the riposte before deciding whether to guffaw or to sneer in the teeth of the responsible.)

'Never mind, so did Shakespeare.' (This is a first-class thing to say as a consolation prize when all are stern. Also it is, of course, always popular to allude to the literature of the realm in which you are extant and Shakespeare will pass for nearly everything.)

On the whole it is the action of he who is slier than his fellows to give the whole sorri business a wide berth. If you try the little game on yourself, you shall undoubtedly place your step on the wrong corn altogether or let slip something improprietorial. English is oh! how an easy language to offend society in as innocently as just-tumbled snow. You chatter in all simple-mindedness and suddenly lo! what a blusching and hostilities and no one will be explanatory.

Vocabular

He who puns – *punster (fem. punstress), pundit.*
In a manner of punning – *punningly, punfully.*
A pun which all repeat – *a current pun.*

Sorts of Fun

Limriks – verses concerning personalities, averring something pretty sarcasticistik.

Praktikal Choke – laying a petti ambusch for some person, such as applestart bed.
Spoonerismus – not for Nordic Students.

Conversation for Occupying Forces
German Army Information Bureau (1940)

During the Second World War when the German Army had reached the French coast and an invasion of Britain seemed imminent in the summer of 1940, a phrase book in German and English was prepared in Berlin for the Nazi troops. Copies of this subsequently came into the possession of British Intelligence from the occupied Channel Islands and revealed typical Teutonic thoroughness in preparing their force for dealing with the English population and their idiosyncrasies. They were to demand that the local population tell them the truth as they overran the nation – and to shoot anyone who told a lie. Here are some typical suggestions:

Are you the mayor?
Open all the cupboards!
Where is the cash?
Write down the amount in the safe.
I shall confiscate all this money!
Show me the way to your house.
I will board and lodge here.
You will wash two shirts, one pair of trousers and three pocket-
    handkerchiefs.
We shall need your horses and carts.
If you drive the wrong way you will be shot.
I have the stomach ache.
I need pills.
Give me opium.

Know Your Comrades in Arms!
Pravda Phrasebook (1948)

In the aftermath of the Second World War when the English and American forces jointly occupied Germany with the Soviet troops, a Russian-English language guide was prepared by the nation's leading newspaper for distribution to the men. Although the booklet provided many useful terms, under-lying some of the phrases was the Russian state's paranoia about the intents of their allies, as this selection of some typical entries shows.

Please give me fried chicks, pulled bread and sower cream.
I would like some curds and one jelly-fish.
How is accommodation for you?
Do you have a bed and room to wash and shit?
I want my hair frizzled.
Do you jerk in your jeep?
Flying in the TU-114 I felt myself excellently.
The woman here are poisonous?
Whose invention is this?
This is a Soviet invention!
How powerful is this reactor?
Shew me a working diagram of this reactor.
Do you have a device for outer space research work?

Instructions for Motorists

Tokyo Information Bureau (1960)

The advent of major tourism from Western Europe and America to Japanese cities inspired several guide and phrase books, which were prepared with painstaking care but an understandable paucity of knowledge of the English language and customs. Nowhere was this perhaps more evident than in the section of the Tokyo booklet about motoring customs in Japanese cities.

At the rise of the hand of policeman, stop rapidly. Do not pass him or otherwise disrespect him.
When a passenger of the foot hove in sight, tootle to him melodiously at first. If the passenger still obstacles your passage, tootle him with vigour and

express by word of mouth the warning, 'Hi! Hi!'

Beware the wandering horse, that he shall not take fright as you pass him. Do not explode the exhaust box at him. Go soothingly by, or stop by the roadside till he pass away.

Give big space to the festive dog that makes sport in the roadway. Avoid entanglement of dog with your wheel spokes.

Go soothingly on the grease-mud, as there lurk the skid demon.

Press the brake of foot as you roll round the corners to save the collapse and tie-up.

Teach Yourself English

Jesus Rodrigues (Rio de Janeiro, 1971)

Brazil – and South America in general – has also seen a huge increase in the number of tourists in recent years and again willing authors and publishers have stepped forward with guidebooks of varying degrees of proficiency. This book, which contained an amazing list of what it described as 'everyday vocabulary' – from 'Easter' to 'strike-breaking' and including 'ostrich', 'pimp' and the even more curious 'forget it' and 'lack of show off' – devoted a section to the country's beautiful girls and their menfolk with an expressive list of phrases in Portuguese and English:

Who is that girl near your brother?
She is a glamour-girl. She has been in the jungle for ten years.
Are the other two fellows connections of hers?
No, one is a big-shot and the other is a cake-eater.
That flapper seems to be a gold-digger – am I right?
That is right. She left the poor boy embroiled.
Is your sister engaged?
Yes, she will be married soon.
Your cousin is chewing the cud.

How is your cousin this morning?

He is completely intoxicated.

John is studying the psychology of the pimp.

Was your sister sick last year?

Yes, that was a case of food-poisoning. She had to be treated for constipation.

Who is the big-shot in this city? Is it that ridiculous knight-errant?

No. Nonetheless, he is the rubber-drive man.

He knows about pill-boxes and sales-drive.

Have you seen the medicine-man in the packing-house?

Have you caught cold, or is it a defluxion?

Neither one. I am tired out.

I would rather have a shorter life than be bald.

Talking in Turkish

Anonymous (1990)

On holiday in Turkey recently I found this little phrase book in a shop and seized on it with all the enthusiasm of a tourist and collector of mangled and misprinted English. It proved to be full of Turkish–English phrases endeavouring to cover every eventuality from making a journey by bus or train, to eating out in restaurants and even being able to cope with an unexpected visit to the dentist. Here are just a few snippets.

You will find in it a choice of remarkable wonks.

I have a request to do you.

How much is it? I'll inke it.

Do not talk on my back.

I am very joyful to have been agreeable to you.

Wait, it comes me an idea.

Whose daughter is orying?

Do you feel any drought?

My nose is nearly frozen.

You have become all pale, I have the quals.

Excuse me, you ave wrong.

What would you do if you were in my place?
I would o so if I was in your plate.

Lexicon Recentis Latinitatis

The Vatican (2003)

This huge Latin tome is probably the largest phrase book ever published. It consists of 23,000 terms spread over 728 tightly packed pages and makes fascinating reading for trivia searchers. Among the more bizarre entries must surely be *sideralis navis* for spaceship, *praecipua scaenica actrix* for a female television presenter, *capsellarum magnetoscopicarum* for a 'video rental shop' and the classic *pastillum botello fartum* to describe the humble 'hot dog'.

Over the years I have collected a number of other curious Latin translations from various books and they will, I think, provide quite enough 'rotten English' for the time being!

Animus imbecillus – An idiotic animal.
Ave, domine – O Lord, I am a bird.
Aves alta petunt – The birds are getting high.
Caesar misit rotundas hominess – Caesar sent round men.
Corvi ovantes gutture – Crows laying eggs in the gutter.
Dulce satis humor – Enough of this sweet humour.
Felices ambo – We all love cats.
In hemicyclio sedentem, ut solebat – Ride a bicycle in order to get warm.
Longius meus – My father.
Nulli secundus – Next to nothing.
Pascebatque suas quisque senator oves – Every senator lived on his own eggs.
Plebs venit ac virides passim dissecta per herbas potat – The crowd lounged everywhere drinking through green straws.
Populissimi – A gathering of happy people.
Receptui cecinit – To sing at a reception.
Sardi venales – Sardines for sale.
Splendide mendax – A first-class liar.

Testudine acta – The tortoise is playing up.

Turpis sine frondibus arbor – A tree is disgraceful without leaves.

Vernit servus tristi vultu – The slave came with a sorrowful vulture.

Vinum amno – I love Venus.

Vomeere findis humum – You are flattening the ground with your stomach.

Eleven

The Tower of Drivel

A Blacklist of Critics' Clangers

Buried in a cemetery at Selborne in Hampshire are the last remains of a critic named Earp whose thoughtless – or perhaps just careless – parents gave him the initials T W. Although there is little evidence to suppose that he was anything other than a quietly spoken, self-effacing man dedicated to his work, his name became the inspiration for the term 'twerp', meaning a foolish person. Earp was a friend of J R R Tolkien and at the university was known as a charming and witty man who belonged to all the art and literary societies. According to one account of his life by Romilly John, he 'took his lack of ambition to the extreme of becoming a critic'. Unlike all of those whose names and words appear in this chapter, however, the unfortunately named T W Earp never delivered a harsh or unkind criticism in his life.

It was the English journalist and wit Sir Sydney Smith who wrote, 'I never read a book before reviewing it; it prejudices a man so.' Benjamin Disraeli, the British Prime Minister and author of several truly awful novels, was just as set in his opinion, famously declaring, 'When I want to read a good book, I write one.' Although I have reviewed only a few books in my life, have from time to time read manuscripts for publishers and passed judgement on their suitability for publication. I am glad to say that – to date – I have not missed a great success like the readers who turned down *Wuthering Heights*, *Lorna Doone*, *The Day of the Jackal* ('it has no reader interest') and the Harry Potter books, before they all became landmarks in literary history.

There are very few things that people have been wrong about as often as they have been wrong about books. In this respect am reminded of one of the highest awards for authors, the Nobel Prize for Literature, which has time and again overlooked great writers. Even when it was first launched in 1901 with such famous men as Henrik Ibsen, Émile Zola, Henry James and Joseph Conrad in their prime, the committee awarded the prize to René Sully-Prudhomme. *René Sully Prudhomme?* Things got no better in the next few years with the award going to Theodor Mommsen, Bjonstjerne Bjornson and Frédéric Mistral, a French poet who wrote only in the Provença dialect. It was not until 1907 that one of the truly great authors was awarded a Nobel Prize – Rudyard Kipling.

In the pages that follow are a selection of critics' clangers voices raised in print against works the writers have adjudged worthless – often very amusingly so – but which time has proved the opposite. Those who were slated have, of course, all had the last laugh . . .

Nothing odd will do long.
　　　　　　　Samuel Johnson on *Tristram Shandy* by Laurence Sterne

So outrageously offensive to reason and common sense that one is naturally led to wonder how it can have been tolerated by a people amongst who astronomy, navigation and chemistry are understood.
　　　　　　　William Cobbett on *Paradise Lost* by John Milton

His principles are ludicrously wicked and his poetry a melange of nonsense, cockneyism, poverty and pedantry.

Charles Lamb on *Prometheus Unbound* by Percy Shelley

Tearing down all shreds of modesty, past all sense of manliness and shame; filthy in word, filthy in thought, furious, raging, obscene.

William M Thackeray on *Gulliver's Travels* by Jonathan Swift

It might have been written by a seamstress who had eaten something too rich for supper and slept upon her back.

Jane Carlyle on *Isabella* by John Keats

I wish her characters would talk a little less like the heroes and heroines of police reports.

George Eliot on *Jane Eyre* by Charlotte Brontë

All the faults of Jane Eyre *are magnified a thousand-fold and the only consolation which we have in reflecting upon it is that it will never be generally read.*

James Lorimer on *Wuthering Heights* by Emily Brontë

Another damned thick, square book! Always scribble, scribble, scribble!

William Henry on *Decline and Fall of the Roman Empire* by Edward Gibbon

I found out in the first two pages that it was a woman's writing — she supposed that in making a door, you last of all put in the panels!

Thomas Carlyle on *Adam Bede* by George Eliot

One must have a heart of stone to read the death of little Nell without laughing.

Oscar Wilde on *The Old Curiosity Shop* by Charles Dickens

If the author cannot think of something better to tell our pure-minded lads and lasses, he had better stop writing for them.

Louisa May Alcott on *Huckleberry Finn* by Mark Twain

His work is evil and he is one of those unhappy beings of whom one can say that it would be better had he never been born.

Anatole France on *La Terre* by Émile Zola

In a hundred years the histories of French literature will only mention it as a curio.

Émile Zola on *Les Fleurs du Mal* by Charles Baudelaire

It is not good enough to spend time and ink in describing the penultimate sensations and physical movements of people getting into a state of rut, we all know them too well.

John Galsworthy on *Sons and Lovers* by D H Lawrence

We fancy any real child might be more puzzled than enchanted by this stiff, overwrought story.

James Lister on *Alice in Wonderland* by Lewis Carroll

In Ireland they try to make a cat clean by rubbing its nose in its own filth. Mr. Joyce has tried the same treatment on the human subject. I hope it may prove successful.

George Bernard Shaw on *Ulysses* by James Joyce

Juvenile trash.

> Edmund Wilson on *The Lord of the Rings* by J R R Tolkien

No, no this kind of thing won't do. The good folks below (I mean posterity) will have none of it.

> James Lowell on *Leaves of Grass* by Walt Whitman

Nothing but two thick tomes in which the author describes the worthless story of worthless people in worthless chatter.

> Edward Engel on *Buddenbrooks* by Thomas Mann

This work is so helpless, so crude, so bad, so clumsily feeble and vulgar.

> Henry James on *An Ideal Husband* by Oscar Wilde

It seemed to me that the man who wrote it had a mind like a sewer. There were few people in this fictional place whose thoughts did not dwell most of the time on booze or lechery or both.

> George Murray on *Under Milk Wood* by Dylan Thomas

A grunt would serve equally well.

> J C Squire on *The Waste Land* by T S Eliot

A huge dose of hyperbolic slang, maudlin sentimentalism and tragic-comic bubble-and-squeak.

> William H Ainsworth on *Moby Dick* by Herman Melville

The critics have never been sure whether the author was trying to truly represent the life of his time or to caricature it — and it seems likely that he has shared their uncertainty.

> Bernard de Voto on *Arrowsmith* by Sinclair Lewis

It is that word 'hummy', my darlings, that marks the first place at which Tonstant Weader Fwowed up.
Dorothy Parker on *The House at Pooh Corner* by A A Milne

It would be useless to pretend that it would be very widely read
Ford Madox Ford on *Heart of Darkness* by Joseph Conrad

The final blow-up of what was once a remarkable, if minor, talent.
Clifton Fadiman on *Absalom, Absalom* by William Faulkner

The physical details, both in lascivious description and implication are disgusting. As to its literary value, I can see none.
Vita Sackville-West on *Lolita* by Vladimir Nabokov

The petty, cowardly, mean and philistine character of the doctor is as alien to the Soviet people as is the malignant literary snob who wrote this book.

V. Semichastny on *Doctor Zhivago* by Boris Pasternak

From the moment I picked up your book until I laid it down I was convulsed with laughter. Someday I intend to read it.

Groucho Marx on *Dawn Ginsbergh's Revenge* by S J Perelman

It is a failure.

Laurence Brander on *Nineteen Eighty-Four* by George Orwell

I would rather put a phial of prussic acid into the hands of a healthy boy or girl than the book in question.

James Douglas on *The Well of Loneliness* by Radclyffe Hall

The book turned out to be a work both disgraceful and scandalous. It abounds in coarse and sometimes disgusting passages and its climax is disgusting. We refuse to print its title or to mention its publishers.

Ernest Oldmeadown on *Black Mischief* by Evelyn Waugh

Readers less easily thrown off their trolley will still prefer Hans Andersen.

R W Lewis on *Of Mice and Men* by John Steinbeck

This rather nasty, rather pompous novel gives us, in all, a precocious small boy's view of life, the boy having been spoiled somehow and allowed to indulge in sulks and tantrums and abundant self-pity.

Walter Inskip on *The Ginger Man* by J P Donleavy

It is only fair to the author to remark on the utter lack of decorum of any kind in this dreadful little volume. The title is meant to be a noun, but I can't help taking it as an imperative.

John Hollander on *Howl* by Allen Ginsberg

Not only is there no word or suggestion of the romantic, sentimental, poetic or spiritual aspects of the sex relation, but it is not even bawdy sex, or comic sex, or sex described with good humour. No glory, no beauty, no stars — just mud.

Thomas Desmond on *Tropic of Cancer* by Henry Miller

The merest trash, not worth a look.

Arthur Forsythe on *Naked Lunch* by William Burroughs

It's a fake — a clever, talented admirably executed fake.

Gore Vidal on *The Naked and the Dead* by Norman Mailer

The author wallows in his own laughter and finally drowns in it. What remains is a debris of sour jokes, stage anger, dirty words, synthetic looniness and the sort of antic behaviour the children fall into when they know they are losing our attention.

Whitney Balliett on *Catch-22* by Joseph Heller

Certainly America has something better to offer the world, along with its arms and its armies, than such a confession of spiritual vacuum as this.

Ambrose Elliott on *From Here To Eternity* by James Jones

We end up by being repelled and by a feeling that it is not quite decent to enjoy so much ugliness and humiliation.

The things worth saving in this book have been degraded almost beyond recognition.
Edmund Wilson on *The Wrong Set* by Angus Wilson

If I were asked to point to a passage
which combined all that prose
fiction should not be — lurid
sentimentality, preposterous morals,
turgid and sticky style — I do not
think I could point to anything
worse than the closing chapters of
this book.
Edmund Gosse on *Howards End* by E M Forster

From time to time it's nice to have a book you can hate — it clears the pipes — and I hate this book.
Peter Prescott on *Breakfast of Champions* by Kurt Vonnegut

A farce that is continually over-
reaching itself. Or, as the Cheyenne
might put it, Little Big Man
Little Overblown.
Gerald Walker on *Little Big Man* by Thomas Berger

The story is too improbable to arouse interest, nor do I like the underlying atmosphere of violence, luxury and lust. I regard it as an obscene book 'liable to corrupt'.
Harold Nicolson on *Goldfinger* by Ian Fleming

One can say of this book — with sufficient truth to make it worth
saying: 'This isn't writing. It's research.'
Stanley Kauffman on *In Cold Blood* by Truman Capote

This book was apparently completed in Cuba in 1960 and, for all the good it is likely to do the author's reputation, it could well have stayed there — permanently.

Geoffrey Wagner on *A Moveable Feast* by Ernest Hemingway

I believe that on the evidence of
this book there is little to say
except that a good wage, accessible
sex and a telly aren't everything.
Any sunday-school teacher could
have made the point in fewer
words.

Fred Majdalany on *Saturday Night and Sunday Morning*
by Alan Sillitoe

The book itself is inaccurate in detail and fraudulent in method to the point of being very bad. The reason these things were not detected by the reviewers is that it said what they wanted to hear.

Martin Green on *The Outsider* by Colin Wilson

For the reader who has put away comic books, but isn't ready for the
editorial in the Daily News.

Gloria Steinem on *Valley of the Dolls* by Jacqueline Susann

He is a good writer, but I wouldn't want to shake hands with him.

Jacqueline Susann on *Portnoy's Complaint* by Philip Roth

That this wretched, drivelling
affair, its impressions fuzzy with
jet lag and neutral-flavoured as an
airline meal, should have been
made into a bestseller, with all the
attendant flimflam of the hired

train and 8.2 autographed copies per minute, is a signpost towards the gap between those who buy books and those who read them.

Jonathan Keats on *Travels* by Edward Heath

It's rare to encounter a novel quite as imaginatively poverty-stricken . . . Combining sentimentality with blokeish guffawing, the author has pioneered a new genre: Mills and Goon.

Peter Kemp on *Man and Wife* by Tony Parsons

One of America's most prestigious mediums for criticism of forthcoming books is the *Kirkus Review*, which is widely respected by authors, publishers and booksellers alike. The magazine recently issued a directive to its critics, 'Editorspeak for a Lovelier Review' (Courtesy of the Copy Desk) which I cannot resist quoting for the sake of anyone who has ever reviewed or been reviewed:

APV	*Pls. Let passive voice be avoided*
AO	*One wishes you'd not use 'one'*
DWT	*Pls. Don't waste my time*
REP REP	*Re-re-repeating yourself; pls. Advance*
FOC, LF	*Need focus, losing foc . . .*
WD?	*Who dis?*
HUH?	*Huh?*
E.G.?	*Can we get an example please?*
EMP	*You gotta **emphasize***
WM?	Um, what means?
WW	Wrong word; find more good one

Twelve

Dying is the Last Thing I Want to Do

A Literary Graveyard of Final Words

Writers have evidently been as keen as anyone among the great and the good to leave a final admonition for posterity. Whether these last words have been especially written to be read after death, committed to a letter or diary, or just imparted on their deathbeds, many have proved revealing and not a few rather amusing. Of course, some authors said nothing, while others of whom greater things might be expected failed to rise to the occasion.

Thomas Gray of *Elegy in a Country Graveyard* fame breathed his last in 1771 with, 'Molly, I shall die,' while the great Samuel Johnson similarly addressed a relative – in his case, his step-daughter – some twelve years later with, 'God Bless you, my dear.' A century on, the French writer George Sand (Amandine Dupon) was a little more fulsome to her family: 'Farewell, I am going to die. Goodbye Lina, goodbye Maurice, goodbye Lolo, good . . .' Then, sadly, she ran out of breath, literally. Another

Frenchman, the grammarian Dominique Bouhours remained true to his profession right to the very end, declaring on his deathbed in 1702: 'I am about to, or, I am going to, die. Either expression is used.' Best, though, I like the story the writer and lawyer, John Mortimer, used to tell of his father, Clifford, also a barrister. The old man's last words were, 'I'm always angry when I'm dying.'

The writers' words quoted in this chapter are taken from a variety of sources from the written to the oral and in many instances are as amusing, satirical and interesting as the people themselves had been in life. The expression which so ideally heads this chapter is attributed to the great American actor John Barrymore, who died in 1942.

Epicurus (*c*. 540–450 BC)

Greek teacher and philosopher who is said to have written over 300 volumes expounding his belief that pleasure was the chief good, of which only one, *Volumina Herculanensia*, has survived.

'Now, farewell, and remember all my words!'

Chrysippus (*c*. 280–207 BC)

Greek philosopher who lived and worked in Athens and is also believed to have been a prolific writer, of which just a few humorous fragments remain.

'Go and give the ass a drink of wine to wash down the figs.'

Niccolò Machiavelli (1469–1527)

Italian author who wrote a number of historical studies, as well as the controversial *The Prince* (1532) which advocated treachery as a means of successful government and was banned by Pope Clement VIII.

'I desire to go to hell and not to heaven. In the former place I shall enjoy the company of Popes, Kings and Princes, while in the latter are only beggars, monks and apostles.'

Pietro Aretino (1492–1557)

Italian poet and adventurer whose controversial verses, the *Sonetti Lussuriosi* (c. 1524), earned him a reputation for impudent wit and the epithet 'the scourge of princes'.

'Keep the rats away now that I'm all greased up.'

François Rabelais (1494–1553)

French satirist who briefly followed careers in the church and medicine before writing a series of riotous, comic masterpieces including *Gargantua* (1532) and *Pantagruel* (1533).

'Ring down the curtain, the farce is over.'

George Buchanan (1506–82)

Scottish reformer and writer who was imprisoned for his satirical poem, *Franciscanus* (1539), directed against the church and renowned for his outspoken history of insurgency among the Scots lords, *Detectio Mariae Reginae* (1562).

'They may leave my corpse to rot where I die if they wish!'

Miguel de Cervantes (1547–1616)

Spanish author, soldier and prisoner of war who was ransomed by monks and went on to create one of the great masterpieces of literature, *Don Quixote* (1605).

'Already my foot is in the stirrup.'

Nicolas Boileau (1636–1711)

French critic whose early satires brought him into trouble with the establishment, but who was ultimately acclaimed for his study, *L'Art Poétique* (1674).

'It is a great consolation to a dying poet to have never written anything against morality.'

William Wycherley (1640–1716)

English dramatist and man about town who became famous for *Love in a Wood* (1671) and *The Country Wife* (1675) and notorious when he took a young wife at the age of 65.

'My dear, you will never marry an old man again!'

Daniel Defoe (1660–1731)

English author whose extraordinary life as a traveller, rebel and government spy inspired his later writings, including the immortal *Robinson Crusoe* (1720) and his roistering tale of low life, *Moll Flanders* (1722).

'I do not know which is more difficult in a Christian life – to live well or to die well.'

Jonathan Swift (1667–1745)

Dublin-born satirist who came to public notice with *Battle of the Books* (1704), but achieved immortality with *Gulliver's Travels* in 1726 – complete with its disguised attack on political parties and religious dissension.

> 'I am dying like a poisoned rat in a hole
> – I am what I am!'

Andrew Bradford (1686–1742)

American writer and in 1719 founder of one of the first magazines in the new colony, the *American Weekly Mercury*, he was later imprisoned for defending the freedom of the press.

> 'Oh, Lord, forgive the errata!'

Alexander Pope (1688–1744)

English satirist, poet and precocious critic of contemporary literature, who was made famous in 1712 by *The Rape of the Lock*.

> '*I am dying, sir, of one hundred good symptoms.*'

Richard Brinsley Sheridan (1751–1816)

Irish-born dramatist and parliamentarian whose hugely popular plays *The Rivals* (1775) and *School for Scandal* (1777) were not sufficient to prevent him from dying in great poverty.

> 'I am absolutely undone.'

Robert Burns (1759–96)

Scottish poet who contributed some of the most beautiful passionate and tender verses in any language including 'Tam o' Shanter' and 'Holy Willie's Prayer'.

'Don't let the awkward squad fire over me.'

William Wordsworth (1770–1850)

English poet whose lifelong love of nature was exemplified in his collections of verse and offset his troubled life and the mental breakdown of his wife, Dorothy.

'Is that you, Dora?'

Sir Walter Scott (1771–1832)

Scottish law clerk who became one of his nation's most famous writers as a result of his series of Waverley novels that mixed country life with high adventure and ranged from the *Legend o Montrose* (1819) to *The Talisman* (1825).

'I have written nothing which on my deathbed I should wish blotted.'

Samuel Taylor Coleridge (1772–1834)

English essayist, critic and poet famous for his verses, notably 'The Rime of the Ancient Mariner' (1798) and 'Kubla Khan' (1816).

'A handsome legacy for that most faithful, affectionate and disinterested servant Harriet Macklin.'

Charles Lamb (1775–1834)

English essayist noted for his reckless humour and wild fun that alternated between tenderness and profound philosophy as demonstrated in collections like *The Last Essays of Elia* (1833).

'My bedfellows are cramp and cough – we three all in one bed!'

Washington Irving (1783–1859)

American novelist whose early worked burlesqued the old Dutch settlers in New York, but who achieved lasting fame with *The Sketch Book* (1819–20) which contained the immortal stories of 'The Legend of Sleepy Hollow' and 'Rip Van Winkle'.

'Well, I must arrange my pillows for another night – when will this end!'

Mary Russell Mitford (1787–1855)

English daughter of a spendthrift physician who turned to writing to support her family and won acclaim for her stories of country life collected as *Our Village* (1832).

'If you wish for another cheerful evening with your old friend, there is no time to be lost.'

Lord George Byron (1788–1824)

Dissipated English poet and 'man of mystery' whose grand tour of Spain, Albania, Greece and the Aegean produced his classic work, *Childe Harold's Pilgrimage* (1812).

'The damned doctors have drenched me so that I can scarcely stand.'

Heinrich Heine (1797–1856)

German author and poet who failed as a banker and doctor before achieving fame as a lyrical and polemical writer with *Das Buch der Lieder* [*Book of Songs*] (1827).

> 'God will pardon me – it's His profession.'

Jules Michelet (1798-1874)

French historian who worked in the Paris Records Office before publishing his monumental 24-volume, *Histoire de France* (1833-67) which he then followed with seven volumes on the French Revolution.

> 'Do you know what linen is? Linen is a great thing – I want to make a book of it!'

Thomas Hood (1799–1845)

English humorist whose popular series of *Whims and Oddities* (1826) led to his editorship of *Hood's Monthly Magazine*. He died curiously, while a mustard plaster was being applied to one of his feet.

> *'There's very little meat for the mustard.'*

Thomas Lovell Beddoes (1803–49)

English poet and physiologist who led a strange peripatetic life as a doctor in Europe until his work *The Bride's Tragedy* (1822) was followed by the even greater success of *Death's Jest Book* in 1849.

> 'I am food for what I am good for – worms.'

Elizabeth Barrett Browning (1806–61)

English poet who wrote a moving epic, *The Battle of Marathon*, while she was only fourteen and later became famous for the heartfelt story of *Aurora Leigh* (1856).

'Beautiful!'

Charles Dickens (1812–70)

English journalist, magazine editor and novelist of innumerable classics including *Martin Chuzzlewit* (1843), *David Copperfield* (1850) and *Little Dorrit* (1857).

'Be natural – for the writer that is natural has fulfilled all the rules of the art.'

Edward Lear (1812–88)

English artist and author whose enduring fame was assured by his illustrated collection of comic verse, *Book of Nonsense* (1846), and its three sequels.

'I did not answer the letters of my friends because I could not write, as no sooner did I take a pen in my hand than I felt as if I was dying.'

Walt Whitman (1819–92)

American poet whose controversial work, *Leaves of Grass* (1855) was labelled 'an indecent book' because of its focus on male love, a taboo subject at the time.

'Oh, dear, he's a good fellow.'

Anne Brontë (1820–49)

English governess and member of the famous family of writers who under her pseudonymn, Acton Bell, wrote *The Tenant of Wildfell Hall* (1848).

'Take courage! Take courage!'

Alice Cary (1820–71)

American poet and storyteller who spent much of her life travelling across America and writing about her experiences and wrote the famous hymn, 'One Sweetly Solemn Thought' with her younger sister, Phoebe.

'I want to go away'

Alfred Williams (1828–1905)

English poet and translator of the ancient manuscript, *The Panchatantra* (c. 200 BC), which included the subsequently much-anthologised stories, 'Leap and Creep' and 'The Three Breasted Princess'.

'My dear, this is going to be a tragedy for us both.'

Jules Verne (1828–88)

French 'Father of Science Fiction' whose prophetic novels *Voyage to the Centre of the Earth* (1864), *From the Earth to the Moon* (1869) and *Twenty Thousand Leagues Under the Sea* (1870) inspired a genre and generations of later writers.

'Are you there?'

Louisa May Alcott (1832–88)

American writer of children's stories that began with *Little Women* in 1868 followed by several sequels, which have delighted countless young readers ever since.

'Is this not meningitis?'

Mark Twain (1835–1910)

American writer and humorist, born Samuel Langhorne Clemens, who was a printer, riverboat pilot and gold miner before achieving fame with the stories of Huckleberry Finn.

'I came in with Halley's comet and I will go out with it.'

Thomas Bailey Aldrich (1836–1907)

American poet, novelist, editor of the *Atlantic Monthly* and author of a bestseller, *The Story of a Bad Boy* (1870), based on his childhood in New Hampshire.

'In spite of it all, I'm going to sleep.'

Émile Zola (1840–1902)

French novelist of the *document humain* that focused on the underbelly of French life in novels such as *Nana* (1880) and *Germinal* (1885). Tragically, he was suffocated by charcoal fumes.

'I feel sick. The dog is sick, too. We are both ill. It must be something we have eaten.'

Ambrose Bierce (1842–1914?)

American writer of sardonic fiction including *In the Midst of Life* (1892) and *Can Such Things Be?*(1893) who disappeared while travelling in Mexico after writing these words.

'To be a gringo in Mexico – ah, that is euthanasia!'

Anatole France (1844–1924)

French writer who began his literary career writing publishers' blurbs and rose to fame with satirical novels such as *Les Opinions de Jerome Coignard* (1893).

'So this is what it is like to die – it takes a long time!'

Paul Verlaine (1844–96)

French poet and short story writer whose life of penury and imprisonment was reflected in volumes such as *Poèmes Saturniens* (1867) and *Élégies* (1893).

'Don't sole the dead man's shoes yet!'

Joel Chandler Harris (1848–1908)

American author who worked as a lawyer and journalist until his comic masterpiece, *Uncle Remus* (1880), made him and his character, Brer Rabbit, world famous.

'I am about the extent of a tenth of a gnat's eyebrow better.'

Sir William Nicoll (1851–1923)

Scottish writer who gave up being a church minister in Kelso to settle in London as an editor and writer on theology and literature for the *Expositor*.

'I believe everything I have written about immortality.'

Oscar Wilde (1854–1900)

Irish wit, poet and dramatist whose notorious life and mastery of the epigram almost overshadow his great works including *A Woman of No Importance* (1894) and *The Importance of Being Earnest* (1899).

'I am dying as I have lived – beyond my means.'

Frank Harris (1856–1931)

Irish-born journalist, incorrigible liar, vociferous boaster and philanderer whose autobiography, *My Life and Loves* (1923–7) was banned for pornography.

'Nellie, my Nellie, I'm going!'

George Bernard Shaw (1856–1950)

Irish novelist, dramatist and critic who worked for a firm of land agents before devoting himself to literature and was propelled to fame by his great philosophical comedy, *Man and Superman* (1902).

'Sister, you are trying to keep me alive as an old curiosity.'

Joseph Conrad (1857–1924)

Polish-born son of a revolutionary who was a merchant seaman for ten years before becoming a famous writer with his novels *Lord Jim* (1900), *Nostromo* (1904) and *Chance* (1914).

> 'I am better this morning. I can always get a rise out of you, Jess . . .'

Sir Arthur Conan Doyle (1859-1930)

Scottish novelist who suffered poverty as a young doctor until his creation of the immortal detective Sherlock Holmes in 1887 in *A Study in Scarlet* made him wealthy and enduringly famous.

> 'You are wonderful.'

Anton Chekhov (1860–1904)

Russian author who began writing comic essays as a student – later published as *Motley Stories* (1886) – but achieved fame as a playwright with several timeless classics including *Uncle Vanya* (1900) and *The Cherry Orchard* (1904).

> '*I haven't drunk champagne for a long time.*'

J M Barrie (1860–1937)

Scottish novelist and dramatist who wrote stories of rural life until the extraordinary success of his social satire, *The Admiral Crichton* (1902), followed by the immortal *Peter Pan* in 1904.

> 'I can't sleep.'

O Henry (1862–1910)

American short story writer who was charged with fraud and fled to Central America, but returned to become a writer in New York where his tales with an unexpected twist – such as *The Four Million* (1906) – made him famous.

> *'Turn up the lights – I don't want to go home in the dark.'*

William Butler Yeats (1865–1939)

Irish writer and poet whose book *The Celtic Twilight* (1893) launched a renaissance of ancient Irish culture and inspired a whole new school of playwrights and poets.

> *'You can refute Hegel, but not the saint or the song of sixpence.'*

H G Wells (1866–1946)

English writer, journalist and prophet whose novels, including *The Time Machine* (1895), *War of the Worlds* (1898) and *The Shape of Things to Come* (1933), have proved hugely influential on the science fiction genre.

'Go away – I'm all right!'

Luigi Pirandello (1867–1936)

Italian novelist and short story writer who became famous for his 'grotesque' dramas, including *Six Characters in Search of an Author* (1920), and who won the Nobel Prize for Literature.

'The hearse, the horse, the driver and – enough!'

Arnold Bennett (1867–1931)

English novelist who began his working life in a solicitor's office but later wrote a series of novels about the 'Five Towns' as well as a number of humorous stories including *The Grand Babylon Hotel* (1902) and *The Card* (1911).

'Everything has gone wrong, my girl!'

Edwin Arlington Robinson (1869–1935)

American poet who won the Pulitzer Prize three times and was widely admired for his novels, notably *The Man Who Died Twice* (1925).

'We'll have our cigarettes together.'

André Gide (1869–1951)

French writer and Nobel prizewinner for his fiction, poetry and plays including the influential *L'Immoraliste* (1902), and his autobiography, *Si le grain ne meurt* (1920).

> *'C'est bien.'*

Hector Munro ('Saki') (1870–1916)

British novelist who became famous as a satirist of the upper-class Edwardian world of England with *The Unbearable Bassington* (1912) and *Beasts and Superbeasts* (1914) but died tragically by a sniper's bullet while serving in the First World War.

> *'Put that bloody cigarette out!'*

Robert Hugh Benson (1871–1914)

English preacher and novelist, author of *Come Rack! Come Rope!* (1921) and the famous ghost story 'The Watcher' (1903).

> 'Arthur! Don't look at me. Nurse!
> Stand between my brother and I!'

Marcel Proust (1871–1922)

French novelist whose semi-invalid life and passion for introspection produced his seemingly endless work, *A la Recherche du Temps Perdu* (*Remembrance of Times Past* 1913–22).

> 'I shall stop now. I can't go on.'

W Somerset Maugham (1874–1965)

English novelist who qualified as a surgeon and used his experiences in the two world wars to produce a series of classic novels including *Of Human Bondage* (1915), *Of Cakes and Ale* (1930) and *The Razor's Edge* (1945).

'Dying is a very dull, dreary affair and my advice to you is to have nothing whatever to do with it.'

Maurice Baring (1874–1946)

English author and journalist who made his name as a war correspondent and for his novels and short stories including the classic, 'Dr Faust's Last Day' (1925).

'Anything you would like me to eat?'

H L Mencken (1880–1956)

American author and critic known as 'The Sage of Baltimore' who edited the fashionable *Smart Set* magazine and contributed to the prestigious work *The American Language* (1936).

'If, after I depart this vale, you remember me and have some thought to please my ghost, forgive some sinner and wink your eye at some comely girl.'

James Joyce (1882–1941)

Irish writer who left Ireland when young but used his native city as the inspiration for a collection of short stories, *Dubliners* (1914), and for his most complex and controversial novel, *Ulysses*, first published in Paris in 1922.

'Does nobody understand?'

Ben Travers (1886–1980)

English novelist and playwright who was a master of the light farce and delighted generations of playgoers with productions such as *A Cuckoo in the Nest* (1925).

'This is where the real fun starts.'

Marguerite Radclyffe Hall (1880–1943)

English novelist whose *Adam's Breed* (1926) won the Femina Vie Heureuse and was followed by her sympathetic study of lesbianism, *The Well of Loneliness* (1928), which was banned for years in Britain.

'What a life!'

Alexander Woollcott (1887–1943)

American journalist, broadcaster and short story writer who is remembered for his larger than life personality and influence on popular tastes.

'I have no need of your Goddamned sympathy – I want to be entertained by some of your grosser reminiscences.'

Donn Byrne (1889–1928)

Irish-American novelist who worked as a cowpuncher in South America, as a garage mechanic in New York and wrote several bestsellers including *Hangman's House* (1926) before dying in a motoring accident.

'I think I'll go for a drive before dinner – anyone coming?'

George S Kaufman (1889–1961)

American humorist and playwright famous for his wit in *The Butter and Egg Man* (1925) and his collaboration with Moss Hart, *You Can't Take It With You* (1936)

'I'm not afraid any more.'

Robert Benchley (1889–1945)

American humorist whose gently sardonic writings were collected in volumes such as *My Ten Years in a Quandary* (1936). He died reading a book called *Am I Thinking?* after writing on the title page:

'No. And supposing you were?'

Dorothy Parker (1893–1967)

American writer famous for her biting wit and satiric humour as exemplified in her collections of verse such as *Enough Rope* (1927) and short stories, *Laments for the Living* (1930) and *Here Lies* (1939).

'Excuse my dust.'

e e cummings (1894–1962)

American writer of essays and poems whose rhythm and style, often omitting capital letters, were seen to great effect in collections such as *The Enormous Room* (1922) and *Eimi* (1933).

'I'm going to stop now – but I'm going to sharpen the axe before I put it up.'

James Thurber (1894–1964)

American journalist and author whose hugely popular comic and satirical books, illustrated by himself, included *Is Sex Necessary?* (1929) and *The Thurber Album* (1952).

'*God Bless . . . Goddamn!*'

F Scott Fitzgerald (1896–1940)

American novelist who lived through the rampant hedonism of the 'Jazz Age' and captured its spirit in *The Beautiful and the Damned* (1922), *The Great Gatsby* (1925) and *The Last Tycoon* (1941).

'Hershey bars will be good enough – they'll be fine.'

Bertolt Brecht (1898–1956)

German dramatist who captured the bawdy and the sublime on paper to make his reputation with *Dreigroschenoper* [*The Threepenny Opera*] (1928), an adaptation of the *Beggar's Opera*.

'*At least one knows that death will be easy – a slight knock at the windowpane, then . . .*'

Thomas Wolfe (1900-1938)

American novelist whose ambitious project for a series of six related novels was cut short by pneumonia, although his reputation was assured by the first book, *Look Homeward, Angel* (1929).

'All right, Mabel, I am coming.'

George Orwell (1903–50)

English novelist who fought in the Spanish Civil War and became a fiery socialist as well as a satirist and made his name with the brilliant *Animal Farm* (1945) and prophetic *Nineteen Eighty-Four* (1949).

> 'At fifty, everyone has the face that he deserves.'

Dylan Thomas (1914–53)

Welsh poet and writer whose talent was revealed in *Portrait of the Artist as a Young Dog* (1940) and *Under Milk Wood* (1954), but whose reputation was ensured by his riotous, drunken lifestyle.

> 'I've had eighteen straight whiskies. I think that's the record. After 39 years, this is all I've done.'

Allen Ginsberg (1926–97)

American poet and angry radical who was one of the leading lights of the 'Beat Generation' and wrote one of its most famous poems, 'Howl', in 1956.

> 'I am quite happy – unaccountably happy!'

Spike Milligan (1918–2003)

Irish author and scriptwriter who co-wrote and performed in *The Goon Show* in 1951, and wrote a number of bestselling books, including a comic gem, *Puckoon* (1963) and a series of 'autobiographies' about his military service, which began with *Adolf Hitler: My Part in His Downfall* (1971).

> 'I told you I was ill.'

Finally, I must just make room for a remark by the great American comedian, scriptwriter and novelist, Woody Allen. Although still very much with us, Woody has already prepared his epitaph:

> 'It's not that I'm afraid to die. I just don't want to be there when it happens.'

Errata

Publishers, Boobs and Apologies

A Gallimaufry of Book Trade Errors

The unprecedented success of *Eats, Shoots and Leaves*, Lynn Truss's book about the vagaries and abuses of the English language, has brought into focus the errors to which writers and publishers are prone. When her little volume began scaling the bestseller lists in 2003, I was reminded of a publisher's advertisement that appeared in an American newspaper in Indiana in the sixties announcing the publication of a book on punctuation. The ad read: 'Revised and enlarged *Rules of Punction*, a valuable, easy-to-understand text for writers, secretaries and students. For a copy send a stamped, self-addressed envelope marked PUNCIATION BOOKLET.' Two errors for the price of one!

Even that revered literary magazine *The Spectator* is not above such errors, as was demonstrated in a review in 1978 which contained the line, 'It does not help that the book is full if misprints and mistakes.' *If* only a proofreader had spotted that

one – but perhaps not one of those who had worked for a large
printing company in Blantyre in Malawi who advertised not so
long ago for 'the services of two fully *qualifeid* proofreaders'
Even more amusing, though, is the unforced error that
appeared in a souvenir handbook published to coincide with
the Wimbledon Tennis Tournament in 1969, which I have to
thank for inspiring the chapter heading. (With a nod to Lynn
Truss, too.) 'We have often in the past had Wimbledon
wobbles,' the anonymous author wrote, 'with nervy players so
shaky that their boobs have sometimes made park club players
blush.' I have no information whether an apology was
demanded or offered.

This final chapter is devoted to a pot-pourri of mistakes
featuring writers and publishers, along with some of the errors
that have bedevilled reviewers of books. It is always easy, of
course, for critics to find faults in a book whether it is in the
writing, the editing or the printing. One man who suffered such
treatment was Sir Max Beerbohm, 'The Incomparable Max', the
writer, critic and caricaturist who died in 1956. His early
parodies in the *The Yellow Book* attracted some hostile reviews
and subsequently brought forth a typically spiky response from
him. For my money, his reply is probably the most effective use
of a comma in all literature: 'It is a pity,' Sir Max wrote, 'that
critics should show so little sympathy with writers, and curious
when we consider that most of them tried to be writers
themselves, once.'

Where better to begin an assortment of errors and misprints
than with a letter to *The Times* written in 1965 by C R Edgeley
the manager of The Times Book Company Ltd:

*Sir, How carefully do people read? The question arises
out of a recent experience here. Not until a copy of a
novel of high literary merit had reached its thirteenth
reader was it noticed that a whole section of the book had*

been erroneously inserted and was, indeed, part of an entirely different book. It is all the more surprising in that, at the point where the wrong insertion is made, the last page of the correct book ended halfway through a sentence, and the first page of the wrong book began a new chapter. The characters and setting were also entirely different.

Easy to Learn Chess published by Max Parrish in 1965 may not have proved quite so easy to readers who were baffled by this explanation at the start of the book:

> *Chess is a game of skill, played by two four smaller squares of equal size, coloured persons on a square board divided into sixty — alternately light and dark.*

Two years later, another London publisher, Macdonald & Co., found themselves in a similarly embarrassing situation when they issued *A Textbook on Climbing*:

> *In climbing, the principal cause of fatigue of the arms is the lack of circulation due to their being held above the head continuously. The feet seldom suffer in this way.*

Following the publication in 1977 of the *Easy Sky Diving Book*, the publishers Warrenton Fauquier of Virginia issued a rather alarming press statement and an insert for every copy of the book. It read:

> *On page eight, line seven, the words 'state zip code' should read — 'pull rip cord'.*

The publishers of the 1978 edition of *Dod's Parliamentary Companion* were also forced to print the following Correction with all copies:

*Reference to Lord Gibson's biography on
page 122: for 'National Front' read*
NATIONAL TRUST.

In 1991, the *Reader's Digest* told the extraordinary story of a
glossy American cookbook which contained a recipe for Silky
Caramel Slice. The instructions stated, 'Put an unopened can of
condensed milk in a pot and leave on the stove for four hours.'
The *Digest* report continued:

> *The publishers later recalled all the books at
> vast expense when they realised they had just
> invented the first exploding pudding. They had
> forgotten to mention that the pot should first be
> filled with water.*

A rather unusual situation faced the *Business Times* of Singapore
when one of their titles in a series of self-help books, *Business
and the Arts*, was issued in 1989:

> *Some readers who called up about the blank space that
> appeared in one of our books published last week were
> inadvertently told to iron the spot and an etching of Ezra
> Pound would appear. The person who gave that
> instruction has since been chastised. It was actually a
> production slip-up. As such, claims for burnt pages and
> damaged irons will not be entertained.*

According to a diary report in the London *Evening News* in 1967
concerning a number of errors found in a recently published
book from a leading publishing company:

> *The publishers have promised to insert a slip in future editions
> acknowledging the sauce of passages quoted.*

The Red Cross Society also had to apologise for a case of the obvious that slipped through in one of their first-aid manuals in 1968:

If the patient faints when standing up he collapses on to the ground.

An even more comic example of the same was reported in 1993 from a handbook issued by the European Parliament in Brussels:

There is a fundamental difference between male and female homosexuality, which is that the former concerns men and the second women.

A corrigendum slip appeared with the copies of the *Australian Dictionary of National Biography* in 2001 referring to page 168:

For 'died in infancy' read 'lived to a ripe old age at Orange'.

Hansard, which records the daily debates in the Houses of Parliament, noted in a totally straight-faced way in May 2003 what was surely the raciest House of Lords Amendment, under the heading 'Baroness Noakes and Lord Astor on the Sexual Offences Bill':

Page 32, line 1, leave out 'genitals', insert 'penis'.

The same august publication was also responsible for another no doubt similarly inadvertent bit of humour in its Index to the 1965 edition:

Seats — see under Members.

* * ! — * ?

She writes rude words for Britain.

Priscilla Quack has a job in publishing. As a trained unexpurgator she works through our backlist of bestsellers and inserts the four-letter words which authors used to indicate with a dash. This makes the new editions more saleable abroad and helps to Close the Gap. Soon Priscilla will be going to work on Dickens. We're proud of our Priscilla.

Rapier and Seedcake, Publishers, Bedford Square, London.

In 1931, the *Washington Post* reported the embarrassment of a local publisher who had issued a new title with the following lines underneath the author's photograph:

> *Words come easy to him — words that have a musical sway, words that come from an active mind, not marital words but those of peace.*

Another American newspaper, *The New York Herald-Tribune* carried this review in its Books Section in 1950:

> This book fills a great gap in public information at a moment when tongues familiar with Sidi Barrani and Derna are looking down the map and wondering how to pronounce Mozambique, Nairobi, Dar es Salaam, Bangassu and Duala.

A lively column known as 'Syndicalism' issued by the American People's Book Series picked up this comic extract in 1954:

> *Man now had his clothes stripped off, and was exposed, naked as when he was born, to the intrusive and penetrating gaze of his brother-man. He had to make new combinations.*

A decade later, the same source found another amusing extract from a review in a literary weekly in November 1964:

> *The volume consists of brief notes and fragments written down at the moment of thought or observation on the back of an envelope, on the soles of his shoes while working in the street.*

A reviewer in *The Observer* discussing *The Major's War* by Alan Perkins in 1967 wrote:

> *Whether shooting his best friend at sea, or in bed with his employer's wife, Ferguson remains the same bowler-hatted and inhibited Englishman.*

The anonymous book reviewer of the *Bournemouth Evening Echo* writing in 1978 about a biography of *Pepys* by Richard Ollard observed:

> *This is not the diary itself, but an account of the man who proved that writing disbars no man from wrenching.*

The Book Column of the *South African Sunday Times* in 1991 carried this wonderful misprint referring to a Catherine Cookson bestseller:

> Her novel, The Rector's Wife was
> topped in the paperback charts in Britain
> last year only by Jilly Cooper's Polo and
> Jeffrey Archer's As the Cow Flies.

In 1970, the editor of the trade magazine *World's Press News*, launched a search to find the world's most prolific author. Under a headline, CHALLENGE, he appealed:

> We believe that Michael Hervey,
> author of 1,500 short stories is the
> prolific storywriter of all time. If
> any other writer, living or dead,
> has equalled this record we shall be
> pleased to hear from him.

The editor of the popular children's comic *Mickey Mouse Weekly* enthused to his young readers in 1959:

> Who hasn't read Lewis Carroll's famous
> classic, and who doesn't love this fabulous
> fantasy? Everyone, I'm sure.

The Sunday Times committed an amusing misprint in its review for a book by Mary Constable in 1958:

> She is a great believer in the importance of a child
> having real knowledge of the body instead of allowing it
> to be wrapped in mystery. She has accordingly included
> in the book an appendix giving clear details of its
> workings.

In 1969, the London *Evening Standard* contacted a number of celebrities to ask what books they were reading. Among these was the millionaire businessman, Charles Clore:

He has just finished Mario Puzo's novel, The
Godfather, *which discusses methods used by
the Mafia. He was most interested.*

Reviewing the *Bedside Guardian 21* in 1970, MP Reginald
Maudling wrote:

*I do not think that I am a very suitable person to
review a bedside book, because my trouble has always
been waking up rather than going to sleep.*

Lloyd's List fell foul of a printer's devil when it reviewed Clare
Francis's *Come Hell or High Water* in 1977:

> The best parts of the book are Clare
> Francis's descriptions of her 'sex
> voyages of discovery', her experiences
> aboard the replica *Golden Hinde*, her
> trip to the ocean bed in the
> submersible *Alvin* and her other visits.

Whether the publisher or author were more embarrassed over
an entry in the Hutchinson & Co Catalogue in 1969 can only be
imagined:

> *The book contains a portrait of the author and
> several other quaint illustrations.*

The following year a novel in the André Deutsch catalogue
suffered from an even more unfortunate error:

*This is the story of four men and a woman, spanning the
years from the height of the war to the present day. It
takes in an underwear hunt . . .*

Sidgwick & Jackson were also hit by a gremlin when publishing *The Professionals: Prostitutes and their Clients* by Iain Scarlet in 1971. Their catalogue stated:

> The Professionals are Alice, Caroline, Jan, Danielle and Kathy. five women to whom prostitution is a business and a way of life. Simon and Joe are the cunters, the men for whom the girls exist.

In 1980, Duckworth provided a similarly unfortunate choice of words about one of their authors:

> *For more than fifteen years, Priscilla Elfrey has specialised in helping managers and executives perform more effectively on the job.*

And just to prove that American publishers can make equally careless gaffs, the 1981 Houghton Mifflin Catalogue commented on one of its authors:

> Lois Lowry is the author of three highly acclaimed children's books, *A Summer To Die*, which won the IRA Children's Book Award . . .

And by way of a typographical break, here is a selection of amusing one-liners from the book trade beginning with an advertisement from the *West Virginia Post* in 1930:

> The Romantic Story of EVANGELINE Henry Wadsworth Longfellow's Immoral Love Epic.

A display advertisement in the *Sussex Herald* in 1948:

> Charles Lending Library. Latest Fiction. No deposit. 3d a weep.

In 1952, a Rangoon newspaper, *The Star,* noticed a promotion sign being used by a major bookshop in the city:

HERE IS A BOOK YOU MUST NOT FAIL TO MISS!

A circular posted through many London doors in 1954 boasted:

We might quote you extracts from our roomful of unsolicited testimonials, but an ounce of fat is worth a ton of fiction.

A London publisher's announcement in 1955:

Forthcoming Handbook HOW I CAN GET AN OLD AGE PENSION. In six volumes. Half-morocco, 143 woodcuts.

Sign in a New York second-hand bookstore in 1961:

Maxwell Bodenheim's A VIRTUOUS GIRL, slightly used. $2.00.

Advertisement from the *Miami Herald,* April 1965:

If you want details of my book HOW TO IMPROVE YOUR MEMORY, send a stamped self-addressed envelope, plus a dame.

A London antiquarian book dealer offered for sale in 1966:

THE SHEPHERD'S GUIDE. A practical treatise on diseases in sheep. Edinburgh, 1807, 8vo, half sheep, worn, uncut, slightly worm.

Time-Life Books encouraged potential readers in 1970:

> You're Invited To Examine THE SEA For 10
> Days With No Obligation To Buy And To
> Receive A Free Gift!

A publisher's announcement for a new title in the *Launceston Examiner* in Cornwall in 1990, declared:

> *Now available fully illustrated – The Complete Cook of Budgerigars.*

And, finally, a small ad in the 'For Sale' section of the *Teignmouth News*, October 2002 offered:

> FULL SET OF ENCYCLOPEDIAS. No longer required
> because partner knows absolutely everything!

In his 'Drama' column in *Cosmopolitan* in April 1980, Peter Freedman wrote:

> Novelist Henry James was never
> much cop as a playwright during
> his lifetime. After his lifetime,
> although his output decreased, his
> theatrical success markedly
> increased with dramatisations of
> his novels penned by others.

This classic literary correction appeared in the much-maligned *Guardian* in September 2001:

> A misprint led Grantly Dick-Read to a novel where a woman was about
> to give birth. The word should, of course, have been hovel.

The normally straight-faced *New Statesman* columnist who signed himself 'Critic' could not resist a wry little footnote in his wartime column at Christmas 1940 after London had suffered several devastating air raids by German bombers:

> *I boast of being the only man in London who has been bombed off a lavatory seat while reading Jane Austen: She went into the bath; I went through the door.*

The *Essex County Standard* revealed another bathroom incident with literary undertones almost half a century later:

> *A distinguished Colchester musician who translated operas while he was locked in railway lavatories for privacy as he commuted to London, has died, aged 72. Mr Tom Hammond, formerly of Mile End, who also wrote an opera himself, became known to train conductors who, it was said, would call out, 'Is that you, Tom?' to which he would reply: 'Yes, I'm just getting through act two.'*

And the controversial contemporary novelist Irvine Welsh kept up the tradition when he was asked in November 2001 by Jack Malvern, diary columnist of *The Times*, how he managed to keep his books so scatological. He replied:

> Well, that's the beauty of laptops. You can type your novels while sitting on the loo and that gives you inspiration.

An unexpected problem with pornography was described by the *Guardian* in 1969:

> *Scotland Yard is searching for more space in which to store its embarrassingly large stock of obscene books and pictures, and HM Customs is forbidden to burn any more*

obscene books because they were breaking the rules of a smokeless zone by making black smoke.

A Scottish sex shop owner, David Cameron, was determined not to have any such issues with pornography, he told Glasgow magistrates in the early seventies. The *Scottish Daily Record* quoted him:

> I am not going to sell dirty books.
> There will be stimulant creams,
> contraceptives, vibrators, pills, sexy
> nighties and artificial sex organs
> – but nothing kinky.

The People reported a case of book promotion gone badly wrong in December 2001, under the headline BOOZE BOOK PLONKER ROW:

> Shocked readers who bought a book on
> how to beat alcoholism discovered a free
> gift – £20 wine vouchers. The promoters
> apologised and withdrew the offer after
> the wife of one alcoholic demanded an
> investigation. Nick Charles, author of
> Through A Glass Brightly, said, 'It
> beggars belief anyone could slip this offer
> into a book like mine!'

The difficulties of first-time novelists are well known, but recently the *Teeside Gazette* came to the aid of one of its readers who was faced with writer's block by appealing for help on her behalf:

> About a third of the way through her book, Mrs
> Sinclair got stuck – and now she is appealing for
> another would-be author to come and help her
> out with the story line. 'The book is about

China's plan to dominate the world,' Mrs Sinclair said.

Finally, probably the ultimate erratum story. It concerns the redoubtable Alice Culpeper, wife and collaborator of Nicholas Culpeper, the seventeenth-century chemist, astrologer and herbalist whose book, *The English Physician Enlarged, or The Herbal*, has never been out of print since first published in 1653. During his lifetime, Culpeper completed 79 books, and after his death Alice did her best to prevent them from being pirated by unscrupulous publishers – in particular one man, Nathaniel Brooke. When, despite protests, Brooke republished Culpeper's *Last Legacy* complete with fake letters of recommendation by the author and his wife, Alice decided the time had come to hit back. She issued an *errata non-corrigenda* of which the ghost of any wronged author would be proud and should serve as a warning to any publisher with similar ideas in mind if there is a feisty widow about:

For Jeers – Read Truth
For Crying Out Against Me – Read Envy
For Raging Against Me – Read Covetousness
For Neglect of My Rules – Read Death of Infants
For Practise Opposing Them – Read Murder

DNE EHT
(Until the next slip of the pen, *nationally*.)

Tell-Tale Piece

Of course, even with all the sophistication of modern printing technology, pens and fingers continue to slip. While this book was going through the checking stage, my editor, Jane Donovan, told me of another unintentional boob in the company's production report that detailed the progress of forthcoming titles. It read: *Ava's Gardener – Her Life and Loves*.

To be sure, there's no guarantee that *something* hasn't slipped past Jane's keen eyes, or those of her copy editor, Sarah Barlow, during the preparation of these pages – though doubtless they will have their excuses ready that they were crying with laughter at the time! In any event, I'd like to invite readers to send me any slips of the pen they may have found in print for a second book. I would even like to encourage my fellow toilers in the gardens of literature who have suffered at the hands of publishers, printers or even – if modesty permits – their *own* fault, to write to me care of the publishers. Let the fun continue!